Distinguished Wisdom Presents . . .
"Living Proverbs"—Vol. 3

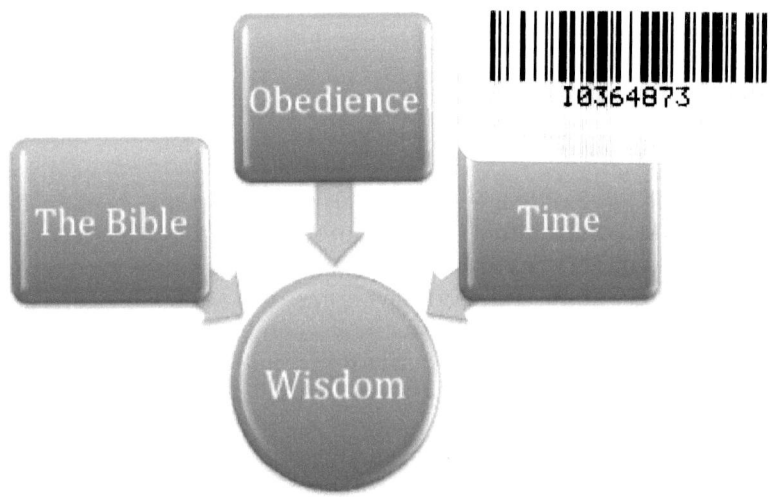

— *Over 500 Wisdom Nuggets
To Enrich Your Life* —

Pastor Terrance Levise Turner, MBA

Well Spoken Inc.| *Nashville, TN*

© 2018 Terrance Levise Turner

All rights reserved. No part of this publication may be reproduced, scanned, transmitted or distributed in any printed or electronic or mechanical forms or methods, including photocopying, recording, or other without prior written permission of the publisher, except in the case of brief select quotations embodied in critical reviews and certain other noncommercial uses permitted by copyright law. For permission requests, write to the publisher, addressed below.

Unless otherwise indicated, all Scripture quotations are taken from the King James Version of the Bible. Unless otherwise indicated all original quotes are those of
Pastor Terrance Levise Turner.

Well Spoken Inc.
P.O. Box 291806 Nashville, TN. 37229
WellSpokenInc@bellsouth.net
www.TerranceTurnerBooks.com

Ordering Information

Quantity sales. Special discounts are available on quantity purchases by corporations, associations, and others. For details, contact the "Special Sales Department" at the address above.

Cover design by Ryan Urz/Susan of LSDdesign/99Designs.com
Book design by Terrance L. Turner

Printed in the United States of America

ISBN	9781732763975	and	9781732763999	paperback
ISBN	9781732763968	and	9781732763982	hardcover

Also by Pastor Terrance Levise Turner:

Distinguished Wisdom Presents... Living Proverbs–Volume 1

Distinguished Wisdom Presents... Living Proverbs–Volume 2

Distinguished Wisdom Presents... The Dynamic Victory Confession: Powerful Confessions For A Victorious Life!

The Earth Is Sad, Little Timmy

Distinguished Wisdom Presents... Your Wealth Is In Your Anointing: Discover Keys To Releasing Your Potential.

This book is dedicated to young people of today, and of future generations. I desire that they have a solid understanding of God and His principles for life and thereby have a successful, prosperous, safe, and godly life.

Contents

Acknowledgements VII
"Living Proverbs"–Vol.3 1
About The Author 252

Acknowledgements

I would like to acknowledge the love and support of my wife, Dr. Avis Turner. She is my partner in life, and the gift that God has given me to help accomplish His purposes in life. Her support and encouragement has helped to enable me to reach the potential God has invested in me. She is a *true* wife. We are better together, and together God is enabling us to reach the world.

Again, I would like to give everlasting thanks to my mother, Geraldine Key, for the foundation of truth and example she laid for my brothers and I. She is the reason I know God as my heavenly Father and the Lord Jesus Christ as my Savior. She continues to be a support and encouragement as I strive to fulfill God's purposes for my life.

I acknowledge the solid example of faith, faithfulness, and morality that I gained from my grandmother, Wilma Starks, and grandfather, Clarence Young. They both were sources of stability in my life. Their examples will continue to live on in all that I do.

I thank God for all the teachers and preachers of wisdom and instruction over my lifetime. My life has been impacted by great leaders in wisdom, instruction, and by example. My mother laid the foundation, and Jehovah God my Heavenly Father has built upon that foundation the right keystones for a successful life.

Preface

My mother introduced my brothers and I, to God as our Father by teaching us the principles of the Book of Proverbs in the Bible. She sat down with us in Bible studies and prayer, and taught us the principles of morality, godliness, and wisdom for life that the Book of Proverbs contained. She took us to church and she lived the principles of God's Word before us in our home. My mother's dedication to the Lord Jesus Christ was my example for seeing how to live a life sanctified unto God. Through her example, along with my grandmother, I gained a deep love for God and His principles.

As I grew up and became an adult, I continued to look to God's Word as the source of wisdom for life. The Book of Proverbs became a mainstay of reliable wisdom for my life. The structure of the book and the manner in which the truths were conveyed were easy for me to digest. They are direct, bite-sized, concentrated nuggets of truth. This affected and helped to craft and shape my thinking.

Distinguished Wisdom Presents... Living Proverbs came into being gradually, day by day. I was led by God to begin sharing the wisdom, which I had learned and ascertained from walking with Him, with others that could be enlighten and encouraged by what was offered.

Living Proverbs came into being in real-time being led by the Spirit and sharing with others what I believed would minister to their lives. My prayer is that they will minister to you now and in time to come.

Introduction

Historical Aspects of Biblical Proverbs

1 Kings 3:4-14 gives the account of King Solomon becoming king after his father King David died. He, though a full grown man, felt as if he was a child in regards to taking over such an immense responsibility to reign as king, especially after such a notable mark, which his father had made on the kingdom of Israel and history.

Solomon prayed to God for wisdom to rule justly and with good understanding for God's people. The following passage describes the account:

> And the king went to Gibeon to sacrifice there; for that was the great high place: a thousand burnt offerings did Solomon offer upon that altar. In Gibeon the Lord appeared to Solomon in a dream by night: and God said, Ask what I shall give thee. And Solomon said, Thou hast shewed unto thy servant David my father great mercy, according as he walked before thee in truth, and in righteousness, and in uprightness of heart with thee; and thou hast kept for him this great kindness, that thou hast given him a son to sit on his throne, as it is this day. And now, O Lord my God, thou hast made thy servant king instead of David my father: and I am but a little child: I know not how to go out or come in. And thy servant is in the midst of

thy people which thou hast chosen, a great people, that cannot be numbered nor counted for multitude. Give therefore thy servant an understanding heart to judge thy people, that I may discern between good and bad: for who is able to judge this thy so great a people? And the speech pleased the Lord, that Solomon had asked this thing. And God said unto him, Because thou hast asked this thing, and hast not asked for thyself long life; neither hast asked riches for thyself, nor hast asked the life of thine enemies; but hast asked for thyself understanding to discern judgment; Behold, I have done according to thy words: lo, I have given thee a wise and an understanding heart; so that there was none like thee before thee, neither after thee shall any arise like unto thee. And I have also given thee that which thou hast not asked, both riches, and honour: so that there shall not be any among the kings like unto thee all thy days. And if thou wilt walk in my ways, to keep my statutes and my commandments, as thy father David did walk, then I will lengthen thy days.

-1 Kings 3:4-14

So, we see that God gave King Solomon wisdom to reign over His people; unlike any other king. The wisdom, which Solomon obtained, was the key to great riches, honor, and renown.

Solomon was a teacher. He was a preacher as well. He taught his sons and others his wisdom using proverbs, parables, and wise sayings. He felt that this was the best way to help those that heard his wisdom to gain the concepts, which he was attempting to convey to their understanding.

In Ecclesiastes 1:1 King Solomon calls himself the Preacher. This is what it says:

> The Words of the Preacher, the son of David, king in Jerusalem.
>
> -Ecclesiastes 1:1

The Book of Proverbs also gives us the biblical purpose of using proverbs, parables, and wise sayings to teach. Proverbs 1:1-7 defines the purpose of the Book of Proverbs, as well as the purpose of this book **Living Proverbs**. This is what it says:

> The proverbs of Solomon the son of David, king of Israel; To **know** wisdom and instruction; to **perceive** the Words of understanding; To **receive** the instruction of wisdom, justice, and judgment, and equity; To give **subtilty** to the simple, to the young man knowledge and discretion. A wise man will hear, and will increase learning; and a man of understanding shall attain unto wise counsels: To **understand** a proverb, and the **interpretation**; the Words of the wise, and their dark sayings. The fear of the Lord is the beginning of knowledge: but fools despise wisdom and instruction.

Pastor Terrance Levise Turner, MBA

-**Proverbs 1:1-7**

Notice, that I bolded a few key words in this passage of scripture, which I would like to point out to you; they clearly explain the purpose of the biblical Book of Proverbs, as well as this book **Living Proverbs.**

The first word that I would like to point out is the Word **know.** *The Strong's Exhaustive Concordance of The Bible* defines this word like this:

> 3045- yada
>
> 1. to know or ascertain by seeing
>
> 2. observation, recognition, instruction
>
> 3. acknowledge, acquainted with
>
> 4. to know assuredly
>
> 5. to be aware
>
> 6. to know for a certainty
>
> 7. to cause to discern
>
> 8. to discover

Therefore, based on these definitions, we see that the initial purpose of biblical proverbs is so that the reader may *know* and ascertain God's wisdom by clearly seeing it. It is to allow the person to observe the deeper meaning of a subject in a condensed way. It is to teach the person how to *recognize*

wisdom when it is being spoken, and to take heed to 'instruction' when it is being given.

The speaking of proverbs is a way of conveying meaning that has been tested and tried as true; and it is a way of conveying those truths to others in a condensed manner that they can gain the certainty of those truths.

They are given so that people can 'discern' truth when it is being presented, without having to have a full explanation. They will not have to have a full explanation in order to discern the meaning that is being conveyed. Proverbs are a condensed conveying of deeper meaning.

The next word, which King Solomon uses to define the purpose of biblical proverbs is **perceive.** This is how the concordance defines it:

> 995-**biyn**
>
> 1. To separate mentally or to distinguish
>
> 2. understand
>
> 3. discern
>
> 4. be cunning
>
> 5. diligently
>
> 6. direct
>
> 7. to have intelligence

8. deal wisely

Notice, the Words used to define perceive are words that deal with the mind. One of the purposes of proverbs of all kinds is for the reader to become more keen in their thinking, and thus, more capable to be successful in life.

The goal is that the person that heeds proverbs will learn to perceive and understand God's ways of doing and being right in life. It is that they will learn to discern right and wrong, as well as timing and manner of doing the right thing.

Through studying proverbs a young person, as well as those more experienced in life, will become more cunning or skillful in navigating decisions, people skills, etc. Various proverbs are given to encourage the reader to become more diligent in life matters; and thus more successful and prosperous.

Short wise sayings, parables, and proverbs can provide swift guidance to a person's decision making. They will direct a person's steps in the midst of a decision making process.

Through heeding various godly proverbs, a person will gain quick intelligence for good judgment. The person that gives themselves to proverbs as a companion to their life will learn to deal wisely in life's diverse situations.

As a person gives themselves to the study of proverbs, they will learn to **receive** wisdom when it is being presented. They will gain more **subtlety** in life. They will become more discreet and refined in behavior and decision-making and

manner; thus, making them better able to smoothly navigate the potentially rough matters of human relationships.

Ultimately, the biblical Book of Proverbs, as well as this book **Living Proverbs** is written so that the person that heeds them may gain a greater **understanding** of God's principles for successful living; and that they will be able to **interpret** God's wisdom as it is presented to them; whether through reading the Bible or in the lessons of life.

This is the purpose of this book **Living Proverbs.** My goal in writing this book is to convey the understanding of the Word of God and God's principles in such a way that it is easy for anyone to understand. My goal is to bring God's Word alive to your understanding.

What Is Wisdom?

What is wisdom? Why is it important? How is it obtained? How is it used?

These are all questions that I will answer for you in this book **Distinguished Wisdom Presents... Living Proverbs-Volume 3**

> Get wisdom, get understanding: forget it not; neither decline from the Words of my mouth. Forsake her not, and she shall preserve thee: love her, and she shall keep thee. Wisdom is the principle thing; therefore, get wisdom; and with all thy getting get understanding.

- Proverbs 4: 5-7

Therefore, we see that the wisdom of God is the number one vital thing that we all need in order to live a successful life. The following scriptures further emphasize the vital importance of wisdom:

> The fear of the Lord is the beginning of knowledge: but fools despise wisdom and instruction.

- Proverbs 1:7

> Also, that the soul be without knowledge, it is not good; and he that hasteth with the feet sinneth.

- Proverbs 19:2

> He that getteth wisdom loveth his own soul: he that keepeth understanding shall find good.

- Proverbs 19:8

Based on these scriptures, we can see that God's wisdom is vital for successful living. The name of this book is **Distinguished Wisdom Presents... Living Proverbs –Vol. 3**, because we must apply God's Word to our daily living in order for it to be beneficial to us.

Habakkuk 2:4b says, **...the just shall 'live' by his faith.** In other words, the only way that the faith and wisdom of the Word of God will work for you is by actually living by what

we learn. As God's Word is lived out in our daily life, it becomes wisdom gained by experience. We are then able to know with certainty, the reliability of God's Word. We can then pass that wisdom on to our family, friends, and those we come in contact with in our daily life.

Wisdom is for success in daily living. These **Living Proverbs** came forth out of my life of seeking to live by God's Word daily. I have dealt with the same challenges that many of you that read this book have had, and I have discovered that *God's Word works for those who work it.*

The Purpose of *Living Proverbs.*

The purpose of *Living Proverbs* is derived from the purpose of my company Well Spoken Incorporated in Nashville, Tennessee. In 2005, God inspired me to start a company with the purpose of communicating the spoken word in a clear, distinct manner that easily conveyed understanding to the listener. We are a publishing company. We focus on biblical material. Well Spoken Inc. is also the company through which I accept professional speaking engagements.

The foundational Scripture that God gave me that inspired the company is Nehemiah 8:7–8. It says,

> Also Jeshua, and Bani, and Sherebiah, Jamin, Akkub, Shabbethai, Hodijah, Maaseiah, Kelita, Azariah, Jozabad, Hanan, Pelaiah, and the Levites, caused the people to understand the law: and the people stood in their place.

> So they read in the book in the law of God distinctly, and gave the sense, and caused them to understand the reading.
>
> — Nehemiah 8:7–8

This particular Scripture indicate that the Levites helped the people to *understand the law of God*, and the people became secure in their place in the land. They became stable as a result of gaining understanding. The Levites read in the book of the law of God *distinctly*, and gave the *sense* or meaning or policy or prosperity of the Scripture. They helped the people to understand what was read. The Levites carried out a specific and importantly vital function so the people would become prosperous through understanding the Word of God that was spoken by the priests.

The Scripture says, *So they read in the book of the law of God distinctly...* From this scripture is where God gave me the name for our brand **Distinguished Wisdom Presents...** The Levites helped the people to *distinguish* what the Word of God was saying or what it really meant. One meaning of the Word distinguish in the Webster's dictionary is *to recognize plainly by any of the senses*. The root meaning is *to prick or pierce apart*. The Word distinct is defined as *clearly marked off; plain; well defined; unmistakable*. God used the Levites to clearly define His Word for the people so that it would be unmistakable what He meant. God wanted them to understand His true purposes for giving His laws, which is for our good.

When God gave me the brand and assignment for *Distinguished Wisdom Presents...* He indicated to me that he had anointed me to share wisdom in a *distinct* manner. Through my study of the book of Proverbs from childhood, I developed a love for wisdom and the Word of God. My education in communications helped to prepare me to speak God's Word. God gave me the name of the company Well Spoken Incorporated as a way of ministering His Word in a clear, specialized manner for those who needed to understand.

I began to share *Living Proverbs* as wisdom nuggets to friends and followers on social media as a means of spreading God's Word to encourage, inspire, and inform. The platform of social media has allowed an expanded reach of God's Word into the world for both believers as well as secular society. God has a need for those who are willing to share his Word with the world. 2 Chronicles 15:3 indicate to us God's need for a *willing vessel* to share His Word. This is what it says,

> Now for a long season Israel hath been without the true God, and without a teaching priest, and without law.
>
> —2 Chronicles 15:3

God needs teaching priests who will teach His Word and bring understanding of His laws to society. This is my purpose, to fulfill God's commission of spreading His Word and ways to the hearts of His people. This book is straightforward. It goes directly into each of the Living Proverbs. They are numbered in order to differentiate one

from the other and also to be able to reference each one individually. They are appropriately supported by rightly applied scripture, which further the readers understanding. The goal of the book is not to develop a new doctrine; rather, it is to *reveal* the wisdom of God that is contained in the written doctrine of Scripture. 3 John 2 says, "Beloved, I wish above all things thou mayest prosper and be in health, even as thy soul prospereth."

Please enjoy this book as a continual companion of counsel and guidance. Meditate on them. Use it as a reference book. With every page you will find a *nugget* of wisdom that will enrich your daily life.

Now delve into the wisdom of God in **Distinguished Wisdom Presents... Living Proverbs –Vol. 3.** *May your life be enriched by the words of wisdom.*

—Pastor Terrance Levise Turner, MBA

"Living Proverbs"–Vol.3

1063. Don't feel bad for someone else's bad behavior. Everyone should take responsibility for his or her own life. It's not your responsibility to take responsibility for someone else. Don't feel bad about someone else's bad behavior.

If thou be wise, thou shalt be wise for thyself: but if thou scornest, thou alone shalt bear it.

—Proverbs 9:12

1064. The rod of correction will keep your children out of the correctional facility.

He that spareth his rod hateth his son: but he that loveth him chasteneth him betimes.

—Proverbs 13:24

1065. Much of religion is fear based, rather than an opportunity for self-actualization. However, God's original plan is for you and me to be all He created us to be. He made us in His image and likeness to act, think, speak, and be like God in the earth. Religion doesn't facilitate that happening. Religion is restrictive, rather than liberating.

Then said Jesus to those Jews which believed on him, If ye continue in my word, then are ye my disciples indeed; and ye shall know the truth, and the truth shall make you free.

—John 8:31-32

1066. When the walls of morality surrounding a nation are broken down, the nation is invaded and trodden down by wild beasts. The land is destroyed and the resources are pillaged.

He that hath no rule over his own spirit is like a city that is broken down, and without walls.

—Proverbs 25:28

1067. It is, what you say it is. You are, who you say you are. You will be, who you declare yourself to be. You have the power to choose the outcome, with your tongue. Declare the truth. Feed on the truth. Be filled with the truth. Become the truth. You are a winner. You are a leader. You are a success. You are blessed. You are highly favored and preferred by God. You are exceptional. You are victorious. You are strong! In Jesus name, amen.

A man's belly shall be satisfied with the fruit of his mouth; and with the increase of his lips shall he be filled. Death and life are in the power of the tongue: and they that love it shall eat the fruit thereof.

—Proverbs 18:20-21

1068. Every victory is a victory toward a greater victory. The best is ahead, and is guaranteed!

They go from strength to strength, every one of them in Zion appeareth before God.

—Psalm 84:7

1069. May we see the glory of who God made us to be in this majestic world, by seeing Him reflected through us in all we do, and by envisioning Christ in us, the hope of glory! Spread your glorious wings in life! It's time to soar!

To whom God would make known what is the riches of the glory of this mystery among the Gentiles; which is Christ in you, the hope of glory.

—Colossians 1:27

1070. I testify, that if you seek the Lord Jesus Christ with all your heart, and make Him your number one thing, living your entire life from the perspective of pleasing Him, He will satisfy your need for friendship, peace, and the blessed assurance of knowing He is always on your side, and living inside of you. He will fight for you. He will comfort you. He will protect you. He will provide for you. In Jesus name, amen.

O God, thou art my God; early will I seek thee: my soul thirsteth for thee, my flesh longeth for thee in a dry and thirsty land, where no water is; To see thy power and thy

glory, so as I have seen thee in the sanctuary. Because thy lovingkindness is better than life, my lips shall praise thee. Thus will I bless thee while I live: I will lift up my hands in thy name. My soul shall be satisfied as with marrow and fatness; and my mouth shall praise thee with joyful lips: When I remember thee upon my bed, and meditate on thee in the night watches. Because thou hast been my help, therefore in the shadow of thy wings will I rejoice. My soul followeth hard after thee: thy right hand upholdeth me. But those that seek my soul, to destroy it, shall go into the lower parts of the earth. They shall fall by the sword: they shall be a portion for foxes. But the king shall rejoice in God; every one that sweareth by him shall glory: but the mouth of them that speak lies shall be stopped.

—Psalm 63

1071. You are a king or queen in God's kingdom. God expects you to take responsibility, and reign in the area of dominion He has allotted to you. Bring order and prosperity to your realm of God's kingdom, by exercising the eternal principles of His royal decree found in 66 books of the Bible. Therein you will find the laws of God's royal rule for His kingdom.

John to the seven churches which are in Asia: Grace be unto you, and peace, from him which is, and which was, and which is to come; and from the seven Spirits which are before his throne; And from Jesus Christ, who is the faithful witness, and the first begotten of the dead, and the prince of the kings of the earth. Unto him that loved us, and washed us from our

sins in his own blood, And hath made us kings and priests unto God and his Father; to him be glory and dominion for ever and ever. Amen.

—Revelation 1:4–6

1072. In order to live a full, rich, and abundant life, you must live your life like a *stingy accountant!* Account for every penny spent. Account for every moment spent.

Be thou diligent to know the state of thy flocks, and look well to thy herds. For riches are not for ever: and doth the crown endure to every generation? The hay appeareth, and the tender grass sheweth itself, and herbs of the mountains are gathered. The lambs are for thy clothing, and the goats are the price of the field. And thou shalt have goats' milk enough for thy food, for the food of thy household, and for the maintenance for thy maidens.

—Proverbs 27:23–27

1073. The key to unbroken success is unbroken focus.

Through desire a man, having separated himself, seeketh and intermeddleth with all wisdom.

—Proverbs 18:1

1074. The key to remaining appropriately happy is to be optimistic and realistic at the same time. You can then remain appropriately balanced, and avoid utter disappointment. Make

plans and expectations from a stable place. You can then plan to take advantage of the true spoils of the realistic opportunity.

Boast not thyself of to morrow; for thou knowest not what a day may bring forth.

—Proverbs 27:1

1075. If you keep on progressing, and keep on confessing, and keep on pressing, you will soon be possessing! Don't give up!

A man shall be satisfied with good by the fruit of his mouth: and the recompence of a man's hands shall be rendered unto him.

—Proverbs 12:14

1076. Do not fear when faced with life's uncertainties. Remain in faith, and do the practical. The power of your faith is greater than your circumstances. Circumstances are subject to change. Faith is the power to change it.

Ye are of God, little children, and have overcome them: because greater is he that is in you, than he that is in the world.

—1 John 4:4

1077. The seed for your future is inside of you. God created you self–contained with everything you need. As you plant

your potential to produce results, through your words, actions, and efforts, you will produce the future you were destined for from the beginning. And, it is very good!

And the earth brought forth grass, and herb yielding seed after his kind, and the tree yielding fruit, whose seed was in itself, after his kind: and God saw that it was good.

—Genesis 1:12

1078. Sometimes *stepping out in faith* is to take the time necessary to get the knowledge needed to make a solid, informed move.

Also, that the soul be without knowledge, it is not good; and he that hasteth with his feet sinneth.

—Proverbs 19:2

1079. The Word works every time, if we will work every time.

For though we walk in the flesh, we do not war after the flesh: (For the weapons of our warfare are not carnal, but mighty through God to the pulling down of strong holds;) Casting down imaginations, and every high thing that exalteth itself against the knowledge of God, and bringing into captivity every thought to the obedience of Christ.

–2 Corinthians 10:3–5

1080. We should seek everyday to fulfill righteousness, by pursuing and living in peace with one another. We should live life to the full in the joy of The Holy Spirit's virtues. We will then be empowered to manifest the wisdom, power, and divine order of God's kingdom on earth. Only through obeying God's divine laws and divine order for living will we have lasting peace, prosperity, and safety.

But seek ye first the kingdom of God, and his righteousness; and all these things shall be added unto you.

—Matthew 6:33

1081. The diamonds are in the details!

Seest thou a man diligent in his business? he shall stand before kings; he shall not stand before mean men.

—Proverbs 22:29

1082. Forget your troubles, and just enjoy the day!

Remember ye not the former things, neither consider the things of old. Behold, I will do a new thing; now it shall spring forth; shall ye not know it? I will even make a way in the wilderness, and rivers in the desert.

—Isaiah 43:18–19

1083. Even wise people sometimes choose to be gullible, and thus suffer the consequences, which is not wise.

A prudent man foreseeth the evil, and hideth himself: but the simple pass on, and are punished.

—Proverbs 22:3

1084. Happy Father's Day to all the good fathers today. If any of you didn't have the benefit of an earthly father in your life, then know for sure that God has been your Heavenly Father. He has provided special attention to your life to make sure you've gotten what you need. So, today, may our greatest thanks go to our Heavenly Father, God Almighty.

A father of the fatherless, and a judge of the widows, is God in his holy habitation. God setteth the solitary in families: he bringeth out those which are bound with chains: but the rebellious dwell in a dry land.

—Psalm 68:5-6

1085. God is your Father today! He loves you! He longs to give you all the blessings He has stored up for you, through His Holy Son, Jesus Christ. Call out to Him today! Ask Him to come into your heart and life, and fill it with all He truly desires for you!

Ask, and it shall be given you; seek, and ye shall find; knock, and it shall be opened unto you: For every one that asketh receiveth; and he that seeketh findeth; and to him that knocketh it shall be opened. Or what man is there of you, whom if his son ask bread, will he give him a stone? Or if he ask a fish, will he give him a serpent? If ye then, being evil,

know how to give good gifts unto your children, how much more shall your Father which is in heaven give good things to them that ask him?

—Matthew 7:7–11

1086. Every reality started as a dream.

For a dream cometh through the multitude of business; and a fool's voice is known by multitude of words.

—Ecclesiastes 5:3

1087. Human knowledge and relative truth will continuously change, fluctuate, morph, and dement overtime. However, the truth of God's Word, the Bible, will remain stable, solid, enduring, and life-giving throughout eternity. It will stand far after the corruptible collapse of the lives and structures built on mankind's carnal ideologies.

Heaven and earth shall pass away: but my words shall not pass away.

—Mark 13:31

For all flesh is as grass, and all the glory of man as the flower of grass. The grass withereth, and the flower thereof falleth away: But the Word of the Lord endureth for ever. And this is the Word which by the gospel is preached unto you.

–1 Peter 1:24–25

Therefore whosoever heareth these sayings of mine, and doeth them, I will liken him unto a wise man, which built his house upon a rock: And the rain descended, and the floods came, and the winds blew, and beat upon that house; and it fell not: for it was founded upon a rock. And every one that heareth these sayings of mine, and doeth them not, shall be likened unto a foolish man, which built his house upon the sand: And the rain descended, and the floods came, and the winds blew, and beat upon that house; and it fell: and great was the fall of it.

—Matthew 7:24–27

1088. Be sure to frame your day around spending time with God through reading the Bible and prayer. Do not limit the Lord to only a small piece, or escape hatch in your life. Rather, make Him the entire frame, foundation, and structure of your life. Then sing praises every morning to be filled with the furniture of The Holy Spirit, which is love, joy, peace, patience, gentleness, goodness, meekness, faithfulness, and self–control.

But the fruit of the Spirit is love, joy, peace, longsuffering, gentleness, goodness, faith, meekness, temperance: against such there is no law.

—Galatians 5:22–23

1089. As you start the day today, know that your Heavenly Father is good. His mercy endures forever, and He loves you! Have a great day!

The Lord is merciful and gracious, slow to anger, and plenteous in mercy. He will not always chide: neither will he keep his anger for ever. He hath not dealt with us after our sins; nor rewarded us according to our iniquities. For as the heaven is high above the earth, so great is his mercy toward them that fear him. As far as the east is from the west, so far hath he removed our transgressions from us. Like as a father pitieth his children, so the Lord pitieth them that fear him. For he knoweth our frame; he remembereth that we are dust. As for man, his days are as grass: as a flower of the field, so he flourisheth. For the wind passeth over it, and it is gone; and the place thereof shall know it no more. But the mercy of the Lord is from everlasting to everlasting upon them that fear him, and his righteousness unto children's children; To such as keep his covenant, and to those that remember his commandments to do them.

—Psalm 103:8–18

1090. The bigger person gives grace. The bigger person gives forgiveness. The bigger person gives patience. The bigger person is more like God. Be the bigger person. Be like God.

Ye have heard that it hath been said, Thou shalt love thy neighbour, and hate thine enemy. But I say unto you, Love your enemies, bless them that curse you, do good to them that hate you, and pray for them which despitefully use you, and persecute you; That ye may be the children of your Father which is in heaven: for he maketh his sun to rise on the evil and on the good, and sendeth rain on the just and on the

unjust. For if ye love them which love you, what reward have ye? do not even the publicans the same? And if ye salute your brethren only, what do ye more than others? do not even the publicans so? Be ye therefore perfect, even as your Father which is in heaven is perfect.

—Matthew 5:43–48

1091. You're a good person. God did a good job in making you, and you've done a good job of making good of what God made!

I will praise thee; for I am fearfully and wonderfully made: marvellous are thy works; and that my soul knoweth right well.

—Psalm 139:14

1092. To open up blinded eyes by faith is a miracle. To restore a missing limb by faith is a miracle. However, to succeed in business or marriage is not a miracle. It is the natural result of working certain reliable principles. We only must be willing and determined to work the principles, and we will obtain miraculous joy and success!

And Jesus said unto them, Because of your unbelief: for verily I say unto you, If ye have faith as a grain of mustard seed, ye shall say unto this mountain, Remove hence to yonder place; and it shall remove; and nothing shall be impossible unto you. Howbeit this kind goeth not out but by prayer and fasting.

—Matthew 17:20–21

1093. Tremendous success usually requires a larger down-payment of effort.

For a dream cometh through the multitude of business; and a fool's voice is known by multitude of words.

—Ecclesiastes 5:3

1094. When something occurs that's not your identity, it's your testimony.

And they overcame him by the blood of the Lamb, and by the Word of their testimony; and they loved not their lives unto the death.

—Revelation 12:11

1095. Prove yourself to yourself, and let everyone else watch you blossom!

For the earnest expectation of the creature waiteth for the manifestation of the sons of God.

—Romans 8:19

1096. If you've been in a process of preparation that seemed to delay, defer, postpone, or hamper the attainment of your desired goal or reward, please be encouraged. God is going to reward you with *"double for your trouble!"* You shall obtain an exceedingly abundant, and great reward that will

more than make up for the pain of delayed dreams! God is blessing you. Be encouraged!

Hope deferred maketh the heart sick: but when the desire cometh, it is a tree of life.

—Proverbs 13:12

For your shame ye shall have double; and for confusion they shall rejoice in their portion: therefore in their land they shall possess the double: everlasting joy shall be unto them.

—Isaiah 61:7

1097. What do you do with faith? You use it to accomplish the necessary things of life.

And the Lord answered me, and said, Write the vision, and make it plain upon tables, that he may run that readeth it. For the vision is yet for an appointed time, but at the end it shall speak, and not lie: though it tarry, wait for it; because it will surely come, it will not tarry. Behold, his soul which is lifted up is not upright in him: but the just shall live by his faith.

—Habakkuk 2:2–4

1098. Money doesn't mean anything to me, but earning it does.

But rather seek ye the kingdom of God; and all these things shall be added unto you. Fear not, little flock; for it is your Father's good pleasure to give you the kingdom. Sell that ye

have, and give alms; provide yourselves bags which wax not old, a treasure in the heavens that faileth not, where no thief approacheth, neither moth corrupteth. For where your treasure is, there will your heart be also.

—Luke 12:31–34

1099. Sleep is coffee for your eyelids. It's best to take it black.

It is vain for you to rise up early, to sit up late, to eat the bread of sorrows: for so he giveth his beloved sleep.

—Psalms 126:2

1100. Praise and worship takes you into another realm. It makes you too high for capture by Satan or demon spirits. Praise and worship causes you to transcend the realm of the flesh. You then enter the realm of God's holy throne!

For thus saith the high and lofty One that inhabiteth eternity, whose name is Holy; I dwell in the high and holy place, with him also that is of a contrite and humble spirit, to revive the spirit of the humble, and to revive the heart of the contrite ones.

—Isaiah 57:15

1101. It takes both the rain and the sunshine to make a life grow. Welcome both as a part of your flourishing future.

In the day of prosperity be joyful, but in the day of adversity consider: God also hath set the one over against the other, to the end that man should find nothing after him.

—Ecclesiastes 7:14

1102. If nothing ever changes, you have to change.

I beseech you therefore, brethren, by the mercies of God, that ye present your bodies a living sacrifice, holy, acceptable unto God, which is your reasonable service. And be not conformed to this world: but be ye transformed by the renewing of your mind, that ye may prove what is that good, and acceptable, and perfect, will of God.

—Romans 12:1–2

1103. "America is good, and if America ever ceases to be good, America will cease to be great. The safeguard of morality is religion, and morality is the best security of law as well as the surest pledge of freedom."

—Alexis de Tocqueville

If my people, which are called by my name, shall humble themselves, and pray, and seek my face, and turn from their wicked ways; then will I hear from heaven, and will forgive their sin, and will heal their land.

—2 Chronicles 7:14

1104. Life is what you look for. If you look for beauty, life is beautiful. If you look for ugly, life is terrible. The wise person takes a realistic view of both, and decides to be happy and effective in light of the entire picture of life.

He that diligently seeketh good procureth favour: but he that seeketh mischief, it shall come unto him.

—Proverbs 11:27

1105. Religion is the bones within the body of belief. It is the structure of behavior through which believers respond to the law. However, without grace, love, wisdom, and discernment, the body is stripped of its life-giving substance, down to a structure of dead bare bones.

Who also hath made us able ministers of the new testament; not of the letter, but of the spirit: for the letter killeth, but the spirit giveth life.

–2 Corinthians 3:6

1106. Success starts as an idea, then proceeds to words, and then ends as deeds.

And the Lord answered me, and said, Write the vision, and make it plain upon tables, that he may run that readeth it. For the vision is yet for an appointed time, but at the end it shall speak, and not lie: though it tarry, wait for it; because it will surely come, it will not tarry. Behold, his soul which is lifted up is not upright in him: but the just shall live by his faith.

—Habakkuk 2:2–4

1107. This is the time to pray. We need the supernatural protection, covering, and intervention of God in our nation and world. If God's people, who are called by His name, will pray and intercede, God will intervene and deliver us.

If my people, which are called by my name, shall humble themselves, and pray, and seek my face, and turn from their wicked ways; then will I hear from heaven, and will forgive their sin, and will heal their land.

—2 Chronicles 7:14

1108. We must choose life in the face of death. We must choose light in the face of darkness. We always have the right to choose.

I call heaven and earth to record this day against you, that I have set before you life and death, blessing and cursing: therefore choose life, that both thou and thy seed may live.

—Deuteronomy 30:19

1109. Life can move along pretty swiftly. One year you're a senior in high school; another year you're senior in college; and the next time you look up, you're a senior!

So teach us to number our days, that we may apply our hearts unto wisdom.

—Psalm 90:12

1110. The only cure for a recurring nightmare is a prevailing dream.

For a dream cometh through the multitude of business; and a fool's voice is known by multitude of words.

—Ecclesiastes 5:3

1111. Don't be in such a hurry that you don't take time to get rest. Even NASCAR drivers take pit stops!

Thus the heavens and the earth were finished, and all the host of them. And on the seventh day God ended his work which he had made; and he rested on the seventh day from all his work which he had made.

—Genesis 2:1–2

1112. Excellence speaks for itself, and it needs no further explanation.

Seest thou a man diligent in his business? he shall stand before kings; he shall not stand before mean men.

—Proverbs 22:29

1113. You know you have matured in walking with God, when you no longer have to do right by persuasion, or by feeling, but you do right by principle.

For when for the time ye ought to be teachers, ye have need that one teach you again which be the first principles of the oracles of God; and are become such as have need of milk, and not of strong meat. For every one that useth milk is unskilful in the Word of righteousness: for he is a babe. But strong meat belongeth to them that are of full age, even those who by reason of use have their senses exercised to discern both good and evil.

—Hebrews 5:12–14

1114. Lucidity means the ability to see things clearly and rationality. It means sanity. God keeps a person's mind in perfect peace, when their mind is stayed on Him. Cast your care on Him, for He cares for you. Rest peacefully tonight, for God gives His beloved children sweet sleep.

Thou wilt keep him in perfect peace, whose mind is stayed on thee: because he trusteth in thee. Trust ye in the Lord for ever: for in the Lord JEHOVAH is everlasting strength.

—Isaiah 26:3–4

1115. May you always have dishes to wash, and trash to take out. In Jesus name, amen.

Blessed be the Lord, who daily loadeth us with benefits, even the God of our salvation. Selah.

—Psalm 68:19

1116. Without action there's no satisfaction. Without action there are no results. Without action there's no fulfillment of the promise!

For as the body without the spirit is dead, so faith without works is dead also.

—James 2:26

1117. If you don't have a clear vision of where you are going, you won't be motivated to get there!

Where there is no vision, the people perish: but he that keepeth the law, happy is he.

—Proverbs 29:18

1118. Almighty, Jehovah God is The Ancient of Days. There is no problem you could possibly have that He hasn't already seen. He's solved your brand of problem millions of times throughout the ages of the human story. So, relax, and cast all your cares upon Him.

Trust ye in the Lord for ever: for in the Lord JEHOVAH is everlasting strength.

—Isaiah 26:4

1119. Diligence is swift insistence on completion of an assigned task in an excellent manner.

The hand of the diligent shall bear rule: but the slothful shall be under tribute.

—Proverbs 12:24

1120. If you receive the images and counsel of the world, it will break your godly focus.

Blessed is the man that walketh not in the counsel of the ungodly, nor standeth in the way of sinners, nor sitteth in the seat of the scornful. But his delight is in the law of the Lord; and in his law doth he meditate day and night. And he shall be like a tree planted by the rivers of water, that bringeth forth his fruit in his season; his leaf also shall not wither; and whatsoever he doeth shall prosper.

—Psalm 1:1–3

1121. It's only what you actually do, that will have eventual value. What you fail to do, forfeits the possibility of an eventual treasure.

Whatsoever thy hand findeth to do, do it with thy might; for there is no work, nor device, nor knowledge, nor wisdom, in the grave, whither thou goest.

—Ecclesiastes 9:10

1122. Overcome the past with a vision of a brighter future.

Where there is no vision, the people perish: but he that keepeth the law, happy is he.

—Proverbs 29:18

1123. Prayer is the infinite God taking time to socialize with finite mankind.

Come unto me, all ye that labour and are heavy laden, and I will give you rest. Take my yoke upon you, and learn of me; for I am meek and lowly in heart: and ye shall find rest unto your souls. For my yoke is easy, and my burden is light.

—Matthew 11:28–30

1124. In most cases, you won't get nearly as much appreciation as you have the opportunity to give. Therefore, you must learn to give freely, with no strings attached, and love by choice.

I have shewed you all things, how that so labouring ye ought to support the weak, and to remember the Words of the Lord Jesus, how he said, It is more blessed to give than to receive.

—Acts 20:35

1125. Lasting love is not falling in love. Lasting love is to walk into love with your eyes wide open, accepting one another, and to make a decision. Then, hold to your commitment. It is the true covenant of marriage.

And he answered and said unto them, Have ye not read, that he which made them at the beginning made them male and female, and said, For this cause shall a man leave father and mother, and shall cleave to his wife: and they twain shall be one flesh? Wherefore they are no more twain, but one flesh. What therefore God hath joined together, let not man put asunder.

—Matthew 19:4–6

1126. Clever is the person who becomes rich from the talents, gifts, and efforts of others, which they do not possess themselves. However, true wealth and wisdom is possessed by the person who discovers, refine, and take possession of the riches he or she contains inside for him or herself.

Wherefore I perceive that there is nothing better, than that a man should rejoice in his own works; for that is his portion: for who shall bring him to see what shall be after him?

—Ecclesiastes 3:22

1127. God's Word doesn't need a co-signer.

Every word of God is pure: he is a shield unto them that put their trust in him. Add thou not unto his words, lest he reprove thee, and thou be found a liar.

—Proverbs 30:5–6

1128. Jesus did not submit to the demands of fear and desperation. Jesus responded to the call of faith in love and power, profusely and decisively, because of His heart of love.

Now a certain man was sick, named Lazarus, of Bethany, the town of Mary and her sister Martha. (It was that Mary which anointed the Lord with ointment, and wiped his feet with her hair, whose brother Lazarus was sick.) Therefore his sisters sent unto him, saying, Lord, behold, he whom thou lovest is sick. When Jesus heard that, he said, This sickness is not unto death, but for the glory of God, that the Son of God might be glorified thereby. Now Jesus loved Martha, and her sister, and Lazarus. When he had heard therefore that he was sick, he abode two days still in the same place where he was. Then after that saith he to his disciples, Let us go into Judaea again. His disciples say unto him, Master, the Jews of late sought to stone thee; and goest thou thither again? Jesus answered, Are there not twelve hours in the day? If any man walk in the day, he stumbleth not, because he seeth the light of this world. But if a man walk in the night, he stumbleth, because there is no light in him. These things said he: and after that he saith unto them, Our friend Lazarus sleepeth; but I go, that I may awake him out of sleep. Then said his disciples, Lord, if he sleep, he shall do well. Howbeit Jesus spake of his death: but they thought that he had spoken of taking of rest in sleep. Then said Jesus unto them plainly, Lazarus is dead. And I am glad for your sakes that I was not there, to the intent ye may believe; nevertheless let us go unto him. Then said Thomas, which is called Didymus, unto his fellow disciples, Let us also go, that we may die with him. Then when Jesus came, he found that he had lain in the grave four days already. Now

Bethany was nigh unto Jerusalem, about fifteen furlongs off: And many of the Jews came to Martha and Mary, to comfort them concerning their brother. Then Martha, as soon as she heard that Jesus was coming, went and met him: but Mary sat still in the house. Then said Martha unto Jesus, Lord, if thou hadst been here, my brother had not died. But I know, that even now, whatsoever thou wilt ask of God, God will give it thee. Jesus saith unto her, Thy brother shall rise again. Martha saith unto him, I know that he shall rise again in the resurrection at the last day. Jesus said unto her, I am the resurrection, and the life: he that believeth in me, though he were dead, yet shall he live: And whosoever liveth and believeth in me shall never die. Believest thou this? She saith unto him, Yea, Lord: I believe that thou art the Christ, the Son of God, which should come into the world. And when she had so said, she went her way, and called Mary her sister secretly, saying, The Master is come, and calleth for thee. As soon as she heard that, she arose quickly, and came unto him. Now Jesus was not yet come into the town, but was in that place where Martha met him. The Jews then which were with her in the house, and comforted her, when they saw Mary, that she rose up hastily and went out, followed her, saying, She goeth unto the grave to weep there. Then when Mary was come where Jesus was, and saw him, she fell down at his feet, saying unto him, Lord, if thou hadst been here, my brother had not died. When Jesus therefore saw her weeping, and the Jews also weeping which came with her, he groaned in the spirit, and was troubled. And said, Where have ye laid him? They said unto him, Lord, come and see. Jesus wept. Then said the Jews, Behold how he loved him! And some of them said, Could not this man, which opened the eyes of the blind, have

caused that even this man should not have died? Jesus therefore again groaning in himself cometh to the grave. It was a cave, and a stone lay upon it. Jesus said, Take ye away the stone. Martha, the sister of him that was dead, saith unto him, Lord, by this time he stinketh: for he hath been dead four days. Jesus saith unto her, Said I not unto thee, that, if thou wouldest believe, thou shouldest see the glory of God? Then they took away the stone from the place where the dead was laid. And Jesus lifted up his eyes, and said, Father, I thank thee that thou hast heard me. And I knew that thou hearest me always: but because of the people which stand by I said it, that they may believe that thou hast sent me. And when he thus had spoken, he cried with a loud voice, Lazarus, come forth. And he that was dead came forth, bound hand and foot with graveclothes: and his face was bound about with a napkin. Jesus saith unto them, Loose him, and let him go. Then many of the Jews which came to Mary, and had seen the things which Jesus did, believed on him

—John 11:1–45

1129. As long as others can make you feel like a visitor, they will prevent you from taking ownership of being at home.

Build ye houses, and dwell in them; and plant gardens, and eat the fruit of them; Take ye wives, and beget sons and daughters; and take wives for your sons, and give your daughters to husbands, that they may bear sons and daughters; that ye may be increased there, and not diminished. And seek the peace of the city whither I have

caused you to be carried away captives, and pray unto the Lord for it: for in the peace thereof shall ye have peace.

—Jeremiah 29:5–7

1130. Your associations will determine your location.

He that walketh with wise men shall be wise: but a companion of fools shall be destroyed.

—Proverbs 13:20

1131. Birds of a feather flock together, and the flock usually ends up in the same place!

He that walketh with wise men shall be wise: but a companion of fools shall be destroyed.

—Proverbs 13:20

1132. If you take time to start something, when there seems to be no apparent reward for it, yet you do it with excellence, because it's the right thing to do, there will be an eventual reward.

Now therefore perform the doing of it; that as there was a readiness to will, so there may be a performance also out of that which ye have. For if there be first a willing mind, it is accepted according to that a man hath, and not according to that he hath not.

−2 Corinthians 8:11–12

1133. Often, how we handle conflict is preparation for promotion.

For promotion cometh neither from the east, nor from the west, nor from the south. But God is the judge: he putteth down one, and setteth up another.

—Psalm 75:6–7

1134. Life never changes. God never changes. Life is full of changes. God never changes. God is faithful for all of life's changes.

There hath no temptation taken you but such as is common to man: but God is faithful, who will not suffer you to be tempted above that ye are able; but will with the temptation also make a way to escape, that ye may be able to bear it.

–1 Corinthians 10:13

1135. The more you give into life the more life gives into you!

There is that scattereth, and yet increaseth; and there is that withholdeth more than is meet, but it tendeth to poverty. The liberal soul shall be made fat: and he that watereth shall be watered also himself.

—Proverbs 11:24–25

1136. We can either work with God to withstand, overcome, and avoid the results of the curse in the earth, by obeying the Bible, or we can disregard His laws and commandments, and suffer the ravages of the curse resulting from sin in the earth. It's our choice.

I call heaven and earth to record this day against you, that I have set before you life and death, blessing and cursing: therefore choose life, that both thou and thy seed may live.

—Deuteronomy 30:19

1137. The lack of money leads to the love of money. As you gain a sincere appreciation of what money can achieve for you, you gain a greater appreciation for it. The lust of money leads to the evils, which occur from those willing to do unlawful things to obtain it. Money is a tool of love from a heart of love. Money is a tool of evil from a heart of evil.

A feast is made for laughter, and wine maketh merry: but money answereth all things.

—Ecclesiastes 10:19

1138. Once you can think your way out, you can work your way out. Riches start with a state of mind.

For as he thinketh in his heart, so is he...

—Proverbs 23:7a

1139. Teach your children the fear of the Lord, so they will have boundaries in their decision-making. Then, even if they make a mistake, they will have a guide to go by, and God's mercy to sustain them.

The fear of the Lord is the beginning of knowledge: but fools despise wisdom and instruction.

—Proverbs 1:7

1140. Whatever you are pursuing, you must allow the heat of your effort to burn out all that is unnecessary, so that all that remains is the gold or silver of your chief definite aim!

As the fining pot for silver, and the furnace for gold; so is a man to his praise.

—Proverbs 27:21

1141. I'm not cooperating with God according to the world's principles or failed religion. I'm cooperating with God according to the principles by which The Ancient of Days has related with man from the beginning of time. If you honor Him, He will honor you.

Blessed is every one that feareth the Lord; that walketh in his ways. For thou shalt eat the labour of thine hands: happy shalt thou be, and it shall be well with thee. Thy wife shall be as a fruitful vine by the sides of thine house: thy children like olive plants round about thy table. Behold, that thus shall the man be blessed that feareth the Lord. The Lord shall bless thee out

of Zion: and thou shalt see the good of Jerusalem all the days of thy life. Yea, thou shalt see thy children's children, and peace upon Israel.

—Psalm 128

1142. Never be overly dependent on another person. No matter who it is. Your *"savior"* is never someone who needs a Savior too. Only Jesus truly saves!

Jesus saith unto him, I am the way, the truth, and the life: no man cometh unto the Father, but by me.

—John 14:6

1143. The key to ongoing success is to do what you know, and to learn what you need to learn.

Give instruction to a wise man, and he will be yet wiser: teach a just man, and he will increase in learning.

—Proverbs 9:9

1144. Don't be afraid to succeed. You can handle all the requirements and demands of your impending success. You were custom-made for your amazing future!

For we are his workmanship, created in Christ Jesus unto good works, which God hath before ordained that we should walk in them.

—Ephesians 2:10

1145. We all start on an equal playing field of time, with 24 hours in a day, 168 hours in a week, and 8760 hours in a year. What will give one person an advantage over another is his or her choice in the use of the time.

So teach us to number our days, that we may apply our hearts unto wisdom.

—Psalm 90:12

1146. A lion is bold enough to attack an elephant when he's hungry!

The wicked flee when no man pursueth: but the righteous are bold as a lion.

—Proverbs 28:1

1147. You can always be promoted to a higher level of doing something, if you're already doing something.

And Jesus, walking by the sea of Galilee, saw two brethren, Simon called Peter, and Andrew his brother, casting a net into the sea: for they were fishers. And he saith unto them, Follow me, and I will make you fishers of men. And they straightway left their nets, and followed him.

—Matthew 4:18–20

1148. The robins hunt when the ground is disturbed.

He that tilleth his land shall have plenty of bread: but he that followeth after vain persons shall have poverty enough.

—Proverbs 28:19

1149. Be faithful. Be consistent. Be patient. You will never get all of life finished in one day. It's ok!

Take therefore no thought for the morrow: for the morrow shall take thought for the things of itself. Sufficient unto the day is the evil thereof.

—Matthew 6:34

1150. A mind that can imagine is still alive!

Where there is no vision, the people perish: but he that keepeth the law, happy is he.

—Proverbs 29:18

And they said, Go to, let us build us a city and a tower, whose top may reach unto heaven; and let us make us a name, lest we be scattered abroad upon the face of the whole earth. And the Lord came down to see the city and the tower, which the children of men builded. And the Lord said, Behold, the people is one, and they have all one language; and this they begin to do: and now nothing will be restrained from them, which they have imagined to do.

—Genesis 11:4–6

1151. In life we can't afford mistakes, but we better save up for them, because we all will make them.

If we confess our sins, he is faithful and just to forgive us our sins, and to cleanse us from all unrighteousness.

–1 John 1:9

1152. The more focused you become on your God-given purpose will cause you to pay less attention to fickle offenses.

Seven times a day do I praise thee because of thy righteous judgments. Great peace have they which love thy law: and nothing shall offend them.

—Psalm 119:164–165

1153. I'm doing what I need to do. I'm learning what I need to do. To do what I need to do!

Wisdom is good with an inheritance: and by it there is profit to them that see the sun. For wisdom is a defence, and money is a defence: but the excellency of knowledge is, that wisdom giveth life to them that have it.

—Ecclesiastes 7:11–12

1154. Rather than to "*boldly go where no man has gone before!*" you should learn what other men and women have already learned, and you will go there too! You can, if you only will!

And that ye study to be quiet, and to do your own business, and to work with your own hands, as we commanded you; that ye may walk honestly toward them that are without, and that ye may have lack of nothing.

–1 Thessalonians 4:11–12

1155. Some things make you famous. Some things make you infamous. Either way, you will be remembered.

When the wicked cometh, then cometh also contempt, and with ignominy reproach.

—Proverbs 18:3

1156. As we look outward, and view the *Olympics* of life, and judge others, may we always look inward, and judge ourselves, and let's go for the gold in life!

Examine yourselves, whether ye be in the faith; prove your own selves. Know ye not your own selves, how that Jesus Christ is in you, except ye be reprobates?

–2 Corinthians 13:5

1157. A world with no boundaries will be like a child with no boundaries: spoiled.

Train up a child in the way he should go: and when he is old, he will not depart from it.

—Proverbs 22:6

1158. Confidence comes from knowledge. Fear comes from ignorance.

Who is as the wise man? and who knoweth the interpretation of a thing? a man's wisdom maketh his face to shine, and the boldness of his face shall be changed.

—Ecclesiastes 8:1

1159. Let our prayers and intercession continue for the families affected by severe weather and flooding. The prayers of the righteous avails much for those hurting. Pray for the protection of those currently suffering in our nation, so that life will be sustained. In Jesus name, amen.

If my people, which are called by my name, shall humble themselves, and pray, and seek my face, and turn from their wicked ways; then will I hear from heaven, and will forgive their sin, and will heal their land.

—2 Chronicles 7:14

1160. You can't predict the day, so you've got to pray!

And he spake a parable unto them *to this end*, that men ought always to pray, and not to faint.

—Luke 18:1

1161. People who don't have a life want to derail yours.

Let a bear robbed of her whelps meet a man, rather than a fool in his folly.

—Proverbs 17:12

1162. Just because you've seen me doesn't mean you know me. Just because you've seen me doesn't mean you've seen me.

Mark the perfect man, and behold the upright: for the end of that man is peace.

—Psalm 37:37

1163. If we hide God's Word, The Bible, in our hearts, God will keep us. He will shepherd us through life. He will protect us. He will sustain us. He will preserve us. In Jesus name, amen.

Thy word have I hid in mine heart, that I might not sin against thee.

—Psalm 119:11

1164. Peace is not the nonexistence of problems. Peace is the refusal to worry, because of the sustaining confidence and rest that comes from reliance upon the unfailing love, concern, power, and attentive commitment of God to help you solve your problems.

Rejoice in the Lord always: and again I say, Rejoice. Let your moderation be known unto all men. The Lord is at hand. Be careful for nothing; but in every thing by prayer and supplication with thanksgiving let your requests be made known unto God. And the peace of God, which passeth all understanding, shall keep your hearts and minds through Christ Jesus. Finally, brethren, whatsoever things are true, whatsoever things are honest, whatsoever things are just, whatsoever things are pure, whatsoever things are lovely, whatsoever things are of good report; if there be any virtue, and if there be any praise, think on these things. Those things, which ye have both learned, and received, and heard, and seen in me, do: and the God of peace shall be with you.

—Philippians 4:4–9

1165. Don't sweat trying to please everyone. People can't even please themselves. If you put a person on a deserted island by his or herself, with all the provisions of life, he or she would still find a way of complaining to themselves about his or herself.

And the Lord said, Whereunto then shall I liken the men of this generation? and to what are they like? They are like unto children sitting in the marketplace, and calling one to another, and saying, We have piped unto you, and ye have not danced; we have mourned to you, and ye have not wept. For John the Baptist came neither eating bread nor drinking wine; and ye say, He hath a devil. The Son of man is come eating and drinking; and ye say, Behold a gluttonous man, and a

winebibber, a friend of publicans and sinners! But wisdom is justified of all her children.

—Luke 7:31–35

1166. Out of our love for God, We should seek to purify our minds, through the washing of the water of the Word of God, the Bible; so as not to offend The Holy Spirit within us. For He continuously hears and sees our every thought, intent, attitude, word, and deed.

And grieve not the holy Spirit of God, whereby ye are sealed unto the day of redemption. Let all bitterness, and wrath, and anger, and clamour, and evil speaking, be put away from you, with all malice: And be ye kind one to another, tenderhearted, forgiving one another, even as God for Christ's sake hath forgiven you.

—Ephesians 4:30–32

1167. You've learned more than most. Now, it's all about making the money. *Doing* is where the money is!

Whatsoever thy hand findeth to do, do it with thy might; for there is no work, nor device, nor knowledge, nor wisdom, in the grave, whither thou goest. I returned, and saw under the sun, that the race is not to the swift, nor the battle to the strong, neither yet bread to the wise, nor yet riches to men of understanding, nor yet favour to men of skill; but time and chance happeneth to them all.

—Ecclesiastes 9:10–11

1168. God knows.

For the Word of God is quick, and powerful, and sharper than any twoedged sword, piercing even to the dividing asunder of soul and spirit, and of the joints and marrow, and is a discerner of the thoughts and intents of the heart. Neither is there any creature that is not manifest in his sight: but all things are naked and opened unto the eyes of him with whom we have to do. Seeing then that we have a great high priest, that is passed into the heavens, Jesus the Son of God, let us hold fast our profession. For we have not an high priest which cannot be touched with the feeling of our infirmities; but was in all points tempted like as we are, yet without sin. Let us therefore come boldly unto the throne of grace, that we may obtain mercy, and find grace to help in time of need.

—Hebrews 4:12–16

1169. God says, "*Yes!*"

For all the promises of God in him are yea, and in him Amen, unto the glory of God by us.

–2 Corinthians 1:20

1170. Often what seems to be the end of the road is actually God putting you on a new road in your life. He's creating a new path for your success. It's a path that He's

paved from before the beginning of time. It's a path to destiny.

Remember ye not the former things, neither consider the things of old. Behold, I will do a new thing; now it shall spring forth; shall ye not know it? I will even make a way in the wilderness, and rivers in the desert.

—Isaiah 43:18–19

1171. Regarding change, choose to live 120 years in a world you help to create!

And the Lord said, My spirit shall not always strive with man, for that he also is flesh: yet his days shall be an hundred and twenty years.

—Genesis 6:3

1172. Just a word of encouragement: Strive to live as long as possible, and make a positive impact on the world in which we live.

With long life will I satisfy him, and shew him my salvation.

—Psalm 91:16

1173. Sometimes it's prayer that helps. Sometimes it's *share* that helps. People need you to talk to God about them, and people need you to talk to them, and share your love, time, and wisdom.

Distinguished Wisdom Presents... "Living Proverbs"–Vol.3

Ointment and perfume rejoice the heart: so doth the sweetness of a man's friend by hearty counsel.

—Proverbs 27:9

1174. You can depend on God's Word that He will never fail you, even when you don't see a sign. His promises in His Word are pure, true, dependable, and undefiled by changing times or meanings. You can confidently depend simply on what God's Word says.

I do set my bow in the cloud, and it shall be for a token of a covenant between me and the earth. And it shall come to pass, when I bring a cloud over the earth, that the bow shall be seen in the cloud: And I will remember my covenant, which is between me and you and every living creature of all flesh; and the waters shall no more become a flood to destroy all flesh. And the bow shall be in the cloud; and I will look upon it, that I may remember the everlasting covenant between God and every living creature of all flesh that is upon the earth. And God said unto Noah, This is the token of the covenant, which I have established between me and all flesh that is upon the earth.

—Genesis 9:13–17

1175. Dream up to the sky, then come back down to earth, and build your dream up to the heavens.

And they said, Go to, let us build us a city and a tower, whose top may reach unto heaven; and let us make us a name, lest we

be scattered abroad upon the face of the whole earth. And the Lord came down to see the city and the tower, which the children of men builded. And the Lord said, Behold, the people is one, and they have all one language; and this they begin to do: and now nothing will be restrained from them, which they have imagined to do.

—Genesis 11:4–6

1176. Keep on toiling with your dream. The Master is aware of your struggle, and most importantly, He is aware of where the *big fish* are! At His Word, be ready to *"launch out into the deep"*, and let down all your "nets" of exercised expertise. You will catch a mighty harvest, and you will be strong enough to gather it all in!

Now when he had left speaking, he said unto Simon, Launch out into the deep, and let down your nets for a draught. And Simon answering said unto him, Master, we have toiled all the night, and have taken nothing: nevertheless at thy word I will let down the net. And when they had this done, they inclosed a great multitude of fishes: and their net brake. And they beckoned unto their partners, which were in the other ship, that they should come and help them. And they came, and filled both the ships, so that they began to sink.

—Luke 5:4–7

1177. Be big! Live to touch the world, and if that's not big enough, create new worlds!

Verily, verily, I say unto you, He that believeth on me, the works that I do shall he do also; and greater works than these shall he do; because I go unto my Father.

—John 14:12

1178. If you help people when you don't have enough, you will help people when you have more than enough. We can always help.

Then Peter said, Silver and gold have I none; but such as I have give I thee: In the name of Jesus Christ of Nazareth rise up and walk. And he took him by the right hand, and lifted him up: and immediately his feet and ankle bones received strength. And he leaping up stood, and walked, and entered with them into the temple, walking, and leaping, and praising God. And all the people saw him walking and praising God: And they knew that it was he which sat for alms at the Beautiful gate of the temple: and they were filled with wonder and amazement at that which had happened unto him. And as the lame man which was healed held Peter and John, all the people ran together unto them in the porch that is called Solomon's, greatly wondering. And when Peter saw it, he answered unto the people, Ye men of Israel, why marvel ye at this? or why look ye so earnestly on us, as though by our own power or holiness we had made this man to walk? The God of Abraham, and of Isaac, and of Jacob, the God of our fathers, hath glorified his Son Jesus; whom ye delivered up, and denied him in the presence of Pilate, when he was determined to let him go. But ye denied the Holy One and the Just, and desired a murderer to be granted unto you; And killed the

Prince of life, whom God hath raised from the dead; whereof we are witnesses. And his name through faith in his name hath made this man strong, whom ye see and know: yea, the faith which is by him hath given him this perfect soundness in the presence of you all.

—Acts 3:6–16

1179. I am slave to no man, and I make no man slave to me.

The rich and poor meet together: the Lord is the maker of them all.

—Proverbs 22:2

1180. After all you've invested, there's nothing left but to succeed. There are no other options, and nowhere else to go. You're *over-qualified* for anything else but the total successful completion of your destiny.

If the clouds be full of rain, they empty themselves upon the earth: and if the tree fall toward the south, or toward the north, in the place where the tree falleth, there it shall be.

—Ecclesiastes 11:3

1181. Make room! You're in the season of multiplication, abundance, and overflow!

Distinguished Wisdom Presents... "Living Proverbs"–Vol.3

Enlarge the place of thy tent, and let them stretch forth the curtains of thine habitations: spare not, lengthen thy cords, and strengthen thy stakes; For thou shalt break forth on the right hand and on the left; and thy seed shall inherit the Gentiles, and make the desolate cities to be inhabited.

—Isaiah 54:2–3

And all these blessings shall come on thee, and overtake thee, if thou shalt hearken unto the voice of the Lord thy God.

—Deuteronomy 28:2

The Lord God of your fathers make you a thousand times so many more as ye are, and bless you, as he hath promised you!

—Deuteronomy 1:11

1182. It is what it is, but you can affect what it becomes.

I call heaven and earth to record this day against you, that I have set before you life and death, blessing and cursing: therefore choose life, that both thou and thy seed may live.

—Deuteronomy 30:19

1183. Life is big. Don't live small.

So that ye come behind in no gift; waiting for the coming of our Lord Jesus Christ.

—1 Corinthians 1:7

1184. Success and progress make you happy!

The desire accomplished is sweet to the soul...

—Proverbs 13:19a

1185. Every life has pleasures and pains. Be thankful to God for the pleasures. Pray to God for the pains. It's all part of a full life.

In the day of prosperity be joyful, but in the day of adversity consider: God also hath set the one over against the other, to the end that man should find nothing after him.

—Ecclesiastes 7:14

1186. Some say we have to "*man-up!*" to deal with the challenges of life, but most importantly, we need to "*God-up!*" Be filled-up with God, so you and I can take on the common problems of mankind in an uncommon, strength-filled manner!

Be of good courage, and let us play the men for our people, and for the cities of our God: and the Lord do that which seemeth him good.

—2 Samuel 10:12

1187. Don't let the devil catch you by surprise. Always pray!

And he spake a parable unto them *to this end*, that men ought always to pray, and not to faint.

—Luke 18:1

Humble yourselves therefore under the mighty hand of God, that he may exalt you in due time: Casting all your care upon him; for he careth for you. Be sober, be vigilant; because your adversary the devil, as a roaring lion, walketh about, seeking whom he may devour: Whom resist stedfast in the faith, knowing that the same afflictions are accomplished in your brethren that are in the world. But the God of all grace, who hath called us unto his eternal glory by Christ Jesus, after that ye have suffered a while, make you perfect, stablish, strengthen, settle you. To him be glory and dominion for ever and ever. Amen.

—1 Peter 5:6–11

1188. Be patient. Be persistent. And you shall prevail!

Fight the good fight of faith, lay hold on eternal life, whereunto thou art also called, and hast professed a good profession before many witnesses.

—1 Timothy 6:12

1189. Greatness is often overlooked, contemned, and misunderstood in its formative or developmental stages. However, God knows how to vindicate greatness and display it as a miraculous sign of His goodness and favor at the appointed time.

And the Lord said, Whereunto then shall I liken the men of this generation? and to what are they like? They are like unto children sitting in the marketplace, and calling one to another, and saying, We have piped unto you, and ye have not danced; we have mourned to you, and ye have not wept. For John the Baptist came neither eating bread nor drinking wine; and ye say, He hath a devil. The Son of man is come eating and drinking; and ye say, Behold a gluttonous man, and a winebibber, a friend of publicans and sinners! But wisdom is justified of all her children.

—Luke 7:31–35

1190. I'm not trying to buy my way into anything. I will earn my way into everything.

Wealth gotten by vanity shall be diminished: but he that gathereth by labour shall increase.

—Proverbs 13:11

1191. When faced with symptoms of sickness, speak to your spirit, because your spirit can revive your body.

The spirit of a man will sustain his infirmity; but a wounded spirit who can bear?

—Proverbs 18:14

1192. Praise and worship are water and refreshing for the soul!

And be not drunk with wine, wherein is excess; but be filled with the Spirit; Speaking to yourselves in psalms and hymns and spiritual songs, singing and making melody in your heart to the Lord; Giving thanks always for all things unto God and the Father in the name of our Lord Jesus Christ.

—Ephesians 5:18–20

1193. Don't complain about being too busy, because life doesn't stop when you're living!

Whatsoever thy hand findeth to do, do it with thy might; for there is no work, nor device, nor knowledge, nor wisdom, in the grave, whither thou goest. I returned, and saw under the sun, that the race is not to the swift, nor the battle to the strong, neither yet bread to the wise, nor yet riches to men of understanding, nor yet favour to men of skill; but time and chance happeneth to them all.

—Ecclesiastes 9:10–11

1194. Focus less on overcoming all of your weaknesses and idiosyncrasies, and invest your full amount of energy and

focus upon fulfilling God's destiny for your life. None of the heroes of faith that were famous in the Bible were perfect. Neither, are any of the modern day ones.

In those days came John the Baptist, preaching in the wilderness of Judaea, And saying, Repent ye: for the kingdom of heaven is at hand. For this is he that was spoken of by the prophet Esaias, saying, The voice of one crying in the wilderness, Prepare ye the way of the Lord, make his paths straight. And the same John had his raiment of camel's hair, and a leathern girdle about his loins; and his meat was locusts and wild honey. Then went out to him Jerusalem, and all Judaea, and all the region round about Jordan, And were baptized of him in Jordan, confessing their sins.

—Matthew 3:1–6

Verily I say unto you, Among them that are born of women there hath not risen a greater than John the Baptist: notwithstanding he that is least in the kingdom of heaven is greater than he.

—Matthew 11:11

Confess your faults one to another, and pray one for another, that ye may be healed. The effectual fervent prayer of a righteous man availeth much. Elias was a man subject to like passions as we are, and he prayed earnestly that it might not rain: and it rained not on the earth by the space of three years and six months. And he prayed again, and the heaven gave rain, and the earth brought forth her fruit.

—James 5:16–18

1195. If your value is based on the opinions of others, your value could quickly decline overnight. If your value is based on the investment that God has put in you, which you have refined, your value will be eternal.

And the multitudes that went before, and that followed, cried, saying, Hosanna to the son of David: Blessed is he that cometh in the name of the Lord; Hosanna in the highest.

—Matthew 21:9

Pilate therefore, willing to release Jesus, spake again to them. But they cried, saying, Crucify him, crucify him.

—Luke 23:20–21

1196. Fear failure enough to succeed. Don't accept it!

Let us therefore fear, lest, a promise being left us of entering into his rest, any of you should seem to come short of it.

—Hebrews 4:1

1197. Do not be discouraged. Don't get used to being sad, because your day of blessing and reward is right up ahead. You will obtain a harvest on the work of your hand. There is hope in your future! Rejoice! The best is still to come!

Thus saith the Lord; Refrain thy voice from weeping, and thine eyes from tears: for thy work shall be rewarded, saith

the Lord; and they shall come again from the land of the enemy. And there is hope in thine end, saith the Lord, that thy children shall come again to their own border.

—Jeremiah 31:16–17

1198. May your diary entries cease to be inspired by your anger over the stereotypical behaviors or failures of those in your past or present. May every stronghold be broken, every curse defeated, and a restoration of the blessing decreed over you and your bloodline from your origin. In Jesus name, amen.

For though we walk in the flesh, we do not war after the flesh: (For the weapons of our warfare are not carnal, but mighty through God to the pulling down of strong holds;) Casting down imaginations, and every high thing that exalteth itself against the knowledge of God, and bringing into captivity every thought to the obedience of Christ.

–2 Corinthians 10:3–5

1199. May you be crowned once again into your place of headship, ruler-ship, honor, and authority. May your esteem be regained worldwide and in the heavens. May God's rule be extended through your exercise of your God–given birthright. In Jesus name, amen.

And God said, Let us make man in our image, after our likeness: and let them have dominion over the fish of the sea, and over the fowl of the air, and over the cattle, and over all

the earth, and over every creeping thing that creepeth upon the earth. So God created man in his own image, in the image of God created he him; male and female created he them. And God blessed them, and God said unto them, Be fruitful, and multiply, and replenish the earth, and subdue it: and have dominion over the fish of the sea, and over the fowl of the air, and over every living thing that moveth upon the earth.

—Genesis 1:26–28

1200. You are a specific, specially designed tool to accomplish a specific, predetermined task at this time in the world. Your task was foreseen by the prescient mind of the all-knowing, almighty God.

For we are his workmanship, created in Christ Jesus unto good works, which God hath before ordained that we should walk in them.

—Ephesians 2:10

1201. God is faithful, even when we don't see a sign of His presence. His Word is true. The just shall live by faith, and not by feelings. God will always come through on His Word. You will come through this season. The Sun is still shining, even as the rain comes down. The Sun's rays will dance upon the raindrops again, proving to you the faithfulness of God.

And he that sat was to look upon like a jasper and a sardine stone: and there was a rainbow round about the throne, in sight like unto an emerald.

—Revelation 4:3

1202. Take a break from the labor of worry today. Cast your cares upon the Lord, for He cares for you!

Come unto me, all ye that labour and are heavy laden, and I will give you rest. Take my yoke upon you, and learn of me; for I am meek and lowly in heart: and ye shall find rest unto your souls. For my yoke is easy, and my burden is light.

—Matthew 11:28–30

1203. Never take a break from prayer, because your adversary the devil never takes a break in seeking to steal, kill, and destroy in your life.

And he spake a parable unto them *to this end*, that men ought always to pray, and not to faint.

—Luke 18:1

Humble yourselves therefore under the mighty hand of God, that he may exalt you in due time: Casting all your care upon him; for he careth for you. Be sober, be vigilant; because your adversary the devil, as a roaring lion, walketh about, seeking whom he may devour: Whom resist stedfast in the faith, knowing that the same afflictions are accomplished in your brethren that are in the world. But the God of all grace, who hath called us unto his eternal glory by Christ Jesus, after that ye have suffered a while, make you perfect, stablish,

strengthen, settle you. To him be glory and dominion for ever and ever. Amen.

—1 Peter 5:6–11

The thief cometh not, but for to steal, and to kill, and to destroy: I am come that they might have life, and that they might have it more abundantly.

—John 10:10

1204. Pray while the waters are still, for you can never predict when the next storm will arise.

And he spake a parable unto them *to this end*, that men ought always to pray, and not to faint.

—Luke 18:1

And the same day, when the even was come, he saith unto them, Let us pass over unto the other side. And when they had sent away the multitude, they took him even as he was in the ship. And there were also with him other little ships. And there arose a great storm of wind, and the waves beat into the ship, so that it was now full. And he was in the hinder part of the ship, asleep on a pillow: and they awake him, and say unto him, Master, carest thou not that we perish? And he arose, and rebuked the wind, and said unto the sea, Peace, be still. And the wind ceased, and there was a great calm. And he said unto them, Why are ye so fearful? how is it that ye have no faith? And they feared exceedingly, and said one to another, What

manner of man is this, that even the wind and the sea obey him?

—Mark 4:35–41

1205. If you do what the Word says, you *are* what the Word says, in spite of what you feel, or how it seems. Also, in spite of who affirms or fails to affirm your identity.

Therefore if any man be in Christ, he is a new creature: old things are passed away; behold, all things are become new. And all things are of God, who hath reconciled us to himself by Jesus Christ, and hath given to us the ministry of reconciliation.

—2 Corinthians 5:17–18

1206. There has been a subtle bomb exploded to the foundations of all that the United States holds sacred. The intent is to see all that this nation stood for slowly crumble to the ground. We must pray for our nation, and for the right candidates to be placed into office.

If the foundations be destroyed, what can the righteous do?

—Psalm 11:3

1207. Move! Sometimes making a decision helps you make a decision. It's helps you to more clearly evaluate your options and clearly discern what you truly want or don't want. And, it

helps you do what you have to do to get it. It helps you get "*un–stuck*" and get on with it in life!

I call heaven and earth to record this day against you, that I have set before you life and death, blessing and cursing: therefore choose life, that both thou and thy seed may live.

—Deuteronomy 30:19

1208. One simple key to greater success is to do what you do well, and do more of it.

Whatsoever thy hand findeth to do, do it with thy might; for there is no work, nor device, nor knowledge, nor wisdom, in the grave, whither thou goest. I returned, and saw under the sun, that the race is not to the swift, nor the battle to the strong, neither yet bread to the wise, nor yet riches to men of understanding, nor yet favour to men of skill; but time and chance happeneth to them all.

—Ecclesiastes 9:10–11

1209. In life, always be willing to put yourself in the other persons' shoes. Consider how they feel, and consider how they got there, and always know that life has another pair of shoes just like theirs, that's just your size!

The rich and poor meet together: the Lord is the maker of them all.

—Proverbs 22:2

1210. Front-load the mighty clouds of blessing with the seeds of good works, tithes and offerings, and faithful love. Then when your season of need arises, your harvest of increase will downpour upon your life in refreshing, replenishing rain.

If the clouds be full of rain, they empty themselves upon the earth: and if the tree fall toward the south, or toward the north, in the place where the tree falleth, there it shall be.

—Ecclesiastes 11:3

1211. Jesus has been healing bodies ever since there have been bodies, and there's nobody He can't heal.

And the whole multitude sought to touch him: for there went virtue out of him, and healed them all.

—Luke 6:19

1212. Continually seek wisdom. Continually listen to instruction. Continually incline your heart and ears to insight. Thereby, if your life begins to drift in the wrong direction, you will be alert enough to hear and see the warning signs, and be able to make adjustments before you have to suffer the consequences.

The ear that heareth the reproof of life abideth among the wise.

—Proverbs 15:31

1213. Pay little attention to little people with little comments about your big dreams and desires. God created you in His image and likeness. You were preordained to prosper, succeed, and accomplish your every predestined dream and assignment in life.

It is naught, it is naught, saith the buyer: but when he is gone his way, then he boasteth.

—Proverbs 20:14

1214. Jump into the biggest pond you can find, and intend to become the biggest fish that the environment can accommodate.

—Alan Weiss, PH.D.

Seest thou a man diligent in his business? he shall stand before kings; he shall not stand before mean men.

—Proverbs 22:29

1215. Whatever may have been your task today, count your day successful if you are better at the end of the day than at the beginning of it. Even if the day ended unlike you wanted, God's mercy is new for you tomorrow.

Blessed be the Lord, who daily loadeth us with benefits, even the God of our salvation. Selah.

—Psalm 68:19

1216. Capture beautiful moments.

Finally, brethren, whatsoever things are true, whatsoever things are honest, whatsoever things are just, whatsoever things are pure, whatsoever things are lovely, whatsoever things are of good report; if there be any virtue, and if there be any praise, think on these things.

—Philippians 4:8

1217. True commitment and a covenant can withstand fluctuating perceptions or fickle feelings.

And he answered and said unto them, Have ye not read, that he which made them at the beginning made them male and female, and said, For this cause shall a man leave father and mother, and shall cleave to his wife: and they twain shall be one flesh? Wherefore they are no more twain, but one flesh. What therefore God hath joined together, let not man put asunder.

—Matthew 19:4–6

1218. Adults are just big children with a nastier bite!

And the Lord said, Whereunto then shall I liken the men of this generation? and to what are they like? They are like unto children sitting in the marketplace, and calling one to another, and saying, We have piped unto you, and ye have not danced; we have mourned to you, and ye have not wept. For John the Baptist came neither eating bread nor drinking wine; and ye

say, He hath a devil. The Son of man is come eating and drinking; and ye say, Behold a gluttonous man, and a winebibber, a friend of publicans and sinners! But wisdom is justified of all her children.

—Luke 7:31–35

1219. Money is not everything, but money does answer all things.

A feast is made for laughter, and wine maketh merry: but money answereth all things.

—Ecclesiastes 10:19

1220. Inoculate your mind from negative influences by taking time to meditate God's word prior to entering a *germy* environment. Then, practice administering periodic full doses internally for safety's sake.

Blessed is the man that walketh not in the counsel of the ungodly, nor standeth in the way of sinners, nor sitteth in the seat of the scornful. But his delight is in the law of the Lord; and in his law doth he meditate day and night. And he shall be like a tree planted by the rivers of water, that bringeth forth his fruit in his season; his leaf also shall not wither; and whatsoever he doeth shall prosper.

—Psalm 1:1–3

1221. In regards to truth, it is better to research, find out, and deal with it truthfully. Rather, than to remain willfully ignorant and continue to suffer the consequences of not knowing.

Give instruction to a wise man, and he will be yet wiser: teach a just man, and he will increase in learning.

—Proverbs 9:9

1222. If you read up, you can lead up, and you can go up.

Buy the truth, and sell it not; also wisdom, and instruction, and understanding.

—Proverbs 23:23

1223. If you show signs that you want to get up, the *hand* will come!

After this there was a feast of the Jews; and Jesus went up to Jerusalem. Now there is at Jerusalem by the sheep market a pool, which is called in the Hebrew tongue Bethesda, having five porches. In these lay a great multitude of impotent folk, of blind, halt, withered, waiting for the moving of the water. For an angel went down at a certain season into the pool, and troubled the water: whosoever then first after the troubling of the water stepped in was made whole of whatsoever disease he had. And a certain man was there, which had an infirmity thirty and eight years. When Jesus saw him lie, and knew that he had been now a long time in that case, he saith unto him,

Wilt thou be made whole? The impotent man answered him, Sir, I have no man, when the water is troubled, to put me into the pool: but while I am coming, another steppeth down before me. Jesus saith unto him, Rise, take up thy bed, and walk. And immediately the man was made whole, and took up his bed, and walked: and on the same day was the sabbath.

—John 5:1–9

1224. Darkness speaks to darkness from a place of darkness, and only leads to further eternal darkness. Light speaks to darkness, and darkness flees!

And the earth was without form, and void; and darkness was upon the face of the deep. And the Spirit of God moved upon the face of the waters. And God said, Let there be light: and there was light.

—Genesis 1:2–3

1225. You're at the precipice of your destiny. Often when you're at the precipice it seems dangerous, but God is faithful. He will never let you down!

Now unto him that is able to keep you from falling, and to present you faultless before the presence of his glory with exceeding joy, To the only wise God our Saviour, be glory and majesty, dominion and power, both now and ever. Amen.

—Jude 24–25

1226. Beauty is in the eye of the beholder. Take time to behold the handiwork of The Lord!

The heavens declare the glory of God; and the firmament sheweth his handywork. Day unto day uttereth speech, and night unto night sheweth knowledge. There is no speech nor language, where their voice is not heard. Their line is gone out through all the earth, and their words to the end of the world. In them hath he set a tabernacle for the sun, Which is as a bridegroom coming out of his chamber, and rejoiceth as a strong man to run a race. His going forth is from the end of the heaven, and his circuit unto the ends of it: and there is nothing hid from the heat thereof. The law of the Lord is perfect, converting the soul: the testimony of the Lord is sure, making wise the simple. The statutes of the Lord are right, rejoicing the heart: the commandment of the Lord is pure, enlightening the eyes. The fear of the Lord is clean, enduring for ever: the judgments of the Lord are true and righteous altogether. More to be desired are they than gold, yea, than much fine gold: sweeter also than honey and the honeycomb. Moreover by them is thy servant warned: and in keeping of them there is great reward. Who can understand his errors? cleanse thou me from secret faults. Keep back thy servant also from presumptuous sins; let them not have dominion over me: then shall I be upright, and I shall be innocent from the great transgression. Let the Words of my mouth, and the meditation of my heart, be acceptable in thy sight, O Lord, my strength, and my redeemer.

—Psalm 19

1227. Just get it done! Just get it done! Don't be an expert in excuses. Just be an expert in results!

Even so faith, if it hath not works, is dead, being alone. Yea, a man may say, Thou hast faith, and I have works: shew me thy faith without thy works, and I will shew thee my faith by my works.

—James 2:17–18

1228. People who get paid big money have proven that they can get results.

Even so faith, if it hath not works, is dead, being alone. Yea, a man may say, Thou hast faith, and I have works: shew me thy faith without thy works, and I will shew thee my faith by my works.

—James 2:17–18

1229. Seemingly little things that you do for seemingly little people can make a big difference and speaks great volumes about your character.

The rich and poor meet together: the Lord is the maker of them all.

—Proverbs 22:2

1230. Be thankful today for all God has given you. Jesus is the answer for all the questions of life. How are you going to

eat? Jesus is the bread of life. How are you going to rest? Jesus is perfect peace. Jesus is all you need for daily living! Enjoy your day today.

Blessed be the Lord, who daily loadeth us with benefits, even the God of our salvation. Selah.

—Psalm 68:19

1231. All the mudslinging in politics leaves both parties looking like pigs. The only answer is to clean up the mess in this nation with real solutions.

Give not that which is holy unto the dogs, neither cast ye your pearls before swine, lest they trample them under their feet, and turn again and rend you.

—Matthew 7:6

1232. One person changed can change the world.

Another parable put he forth unto them, saying, The kingdom of heaven is like to a grain of mustard seed, which a man took, and sowed in his field: which indeed is the least of all seeds: but when it is grown, it is the greatest among herbs, and becometh a tree, so that the birds of the air come and lodge in the branches thereof. Another parable spake he unto them; The kingdom of heaven is like unto leaven, which a woman took, and hid in three measures of meal, till the whole was leavened.

—Matthew 13:31–33

1233. Every step forward is a step in the right direction.

The steps of a good man are ordered by the Lord: and he delighteth in his way.

—Psalm 37:23

1234. If you truly recognize your value, you can make hundreds of thousands of dollars in your profession, but you can make millions of dollars in your gifts and talents.

Every man also to whom God hath given riches and wealth, and hath given him power to eat thereof, and to take his portion, and to rejoice in his labour; this is the gift of God.

—Ecclesiastes 5:19

1235. A lot of people look at safety and safe trips, and safe days on the road, and in other places, as commonplace, and without taking time to be thankful, but one thing we must realize is that death is commonplace. Therefore, we should be thankful every day for God's mercy.

So teach us to number our days, that we may apply our hearts unto wisdom.

—Psalm 90:12

1236. When you've had enough of not having enough, you will discipline your life to have more than enough.

In all labour there is profit: but the talk of the lips tendeth only to penury.

—Proverbs 14:23

1237. When you know who you are, no one can stop the force of who you are, and the force of who you are will change your whole situation.

But let every man prove his own work, and then shall he have rejoicing in himself alone, and not in another.

—Galatians 6:4

1238. When people get to the end of their rope, they are always looking for hope, even those who seem so self-assured, as if they don't need it.

Then Agrippa said unto Paul, Almost thou persuadest me to be a Christian.

—Acts 26:28

1239. Every time you successfully face your fears, and overcome them, you become more fearless.

Fear thou not; for I am with thee: be not dismayed; for I am thy God: I will strengthen thee; yea, I will help thee; yea, I will uphold thee with the right hand of my righteousness.

—Isaiah 41:10

1240. Pray in faith. Then, rest in trust.

But when Jesus heard it, he answered him, saying, Fear not: believe only, and she shall be made whole.

—Luke 8:50

1241. The wrong conversations with the wrong people can cause you to make the wrong decisions. Never listen to people who have a lower perspective of life and it's potential, in order to discuss your future. They can only advise you as far and high as they can see. Talk to failures about failure. Then, avoid it. Talk to successes about success. Then, embrace it.

He that walketh with wise men shall be wise: but a companion of fools shall be destroyed.

—Proverbs 13:20

1242. People who have money had a large perspective before they got money, and that's why they have money now!

For as he thinketh in his heart, so is he...

—Proverbs 23:7a

And God gave Solomon wisdom and understanding exceeding much, and largeness of heart, even as the sand that is on the sea shore.

—1 Kings 4:29

And the king made silver and gold at Jerusalem as plenteous as stones, and cedar trees made he as the sycamore trees that are in the vale for abundance.

—2 Chronicles 1:15

1243. Intelligence does not result from education, but the attainment of education results from being intelligent.

Give instruction to a wise man, and he will be yet wiser: teach a just man, and he will increase in learning.

—Proverbs 9:9

1244. Some people have developed the *art* of wasting time, like sitting for hours eating dinner and talking, laughing, and drinking coffee, or, sitting around watching television programs, one after another. I know there must be value in that lifestyle, like better relationships. However, when you are in a hurry to succeed, accomplish, and fulfill your destiny, it's an *art* that takes effort to acquire.

In the morning sow thy seed, and in the evening withhold not thine hand: for thou knowest not whether shall prosper, either this or that, or whether they both shall be alike good.

—Ecclesiastes 11:6

1245. Don't feel bad about being in a learning process toward greater success. If you are studying the right things and are progressing in the right direction, you are already a

success. You are many paces ahead of those who are sitting still. Be encouraged. Success takes time and progressive effort.

If ye be willing and obedient, ye shall eat the good of the land.

—Isaiah 1:19

1246. Sometimes church is not about religion, but it is about a tradition of good, wholesome living. It's about a community of believers, (people who believe the same thing), being willing to join together to support one another, encourage one another, and are glad to see one another. Church is about good, wholesome living!

Not forsaking the assembling of ourselves together, as the manner of some is; but exhorting one another: and so much the more, as ye see the day approaching.

—Hebrews 10:25

1247. The Lord is working on your behalf this week. You are blessed, blessed, blessed! Oh, so blessed! The Lord is working on your behalf! Accept it by faith. In Jesus name, amen!

And we know that all things work together for good to them that love God, to them who are the called according to his purpose.

—Romans 8:28

1248. Allow the Words of love, peace, hope, and joy to inspire your soul and spirit! To *inspire* means to breathe in. Allow God's life-giving music to be breathed into your soul. You will be revived!

And the Lord God formed man of the dust of the ground, and breathed into his nostrils the breath of life; and man became a living soul.

—Genesis 2:7

1249. As you lie down tonight, be at peace. God is sovereign. He is well able to hold the world up while you sleep. He will keep you in perfect peace as you keep your mind stayed on Him and rest and rely upon Him.

It is vain for you to rise up early, to sit up late, to eat the bread of sorrows: for so he giveth his beloved sleep.

—Psalm 127:2

1250. Pray and vote. Vote and pray. We must fulfill our civic responsibility to vote. We must fulfill our spiritual responsibility to pray, because we don't truly know what either candidate will do once they actually get into office. We simply must look at their track record and platform, and see how closely it lines up with our belief system. Then, vote in faith, stay involved, and leave the rest to God.

I exhort therefore, that, first of all, supplications, prayers, intercessions, and giving of thanks, be made for all men; For

kings, and for all that are in authority; that we may lead a quiet and peaceable life in all godliness and honesty.

—1 Timothy 2:1–2

1251. Rather than spending your days fighting enemies, spend your days pleasing God by operating excellently in your God–given task or assignment. Then, leave your enemies in the hand of The Lord. The sound of your success will drown out the distraction of barking dogs!

When a man's ways please the Lord, he maketh even his enemies to be at peace with him.

—Proverbs 16:7

1252. If you feel like you've been running and running just to get to the starting line, don't be discouraged. You are now ready to win the race of destiny fully prepared for all the rigors of the race. So, ready! Set! Go! Your destiny is waiting!

Know ye not that they which run in a race run all, but one receiveth the prize? So run, that ye may obtain. And every man that striveth for the mastery is temperate in all things. Now they do it to obtain a corruptible crown; but we an incorruptible. I therefore so run, not as uncertainly; so fight I, not as one that beateth the air: But I keep under my body, and bring it into subjection: lest that by any means, when I have preached to others, I myself should be a castaway.

—1 Corinthians 9:24–27

1253. One of the keys to a husband's success is to have a wife with a large enough capacity to follow big dreams and willingness to trust the direction that her husband leads. This is always easier if she is made confident that the husband is following a bigger God than himself.

Whoso findeth a wife findeth a good thing, and obtaineth favour of the Lord.

—Proverbs 18:22

1254. Crime doesn't have a color. Poverty doesn't have a color. However, racism is often activated by color. Solve the problems that do not have a color for everyone. Then, you will be better able to clearly see the problems that are activated by blatant racism.

Let every soul be subject unto the higher powers. For there is no power but of God: the powers that be are ordained of God. Whosoever therefore resisteth the power, resisteth the ordinance of God: and they that resist shall receive to themselves damnation. For rulers are not a terror to good works, but to the evil. Wilt thou then not be afraid of the power? do that which is good, and thou shalt have praise of the same: for he is the minister of God to thee for good. But if thou do that which is evil, be afraid; for he beareth not the sword in vain: for he is the minister of God, a revenger to execute wrath upon him that doeth evil. Wherefore ye must needs be subject, not only for wrath, but also for conscience sake.

—Romans 13:1-5

But he that doeth wrong shall receive for the wrong which he hath done: and there is no respect of persons.

—Colossians 3:25

1255. There are some people who talk, and you recognize they are talking. But, there are some people who talk and you listen. Substance, sincerity, and believability make the difference.

The simple believeth every word: but the prudent man looketh well to his going.

—Proverbs 14:15

1256. If you are big inside, everything around you will grow.

For as he thinketh in his heart, so is he...

—Proverbs 23:7a

And God gave Solomon wisdom and understanding exceeding much, and largeness of heart, even as the sand that is on the sea shore.

—1 Kings 4:29

And the king made silver and gold at Jerusalem as plenteous as stones, and cedar trees made he as the sycomore trees that are in the vale for abundance.

–2 Chronicles 1:15

1257. Dreams are difficult, disappointing, and discouraging. However, if you endure unto the end you will receive the crown.

Hope deferred maketh the heart sick: but when the desire cometh, it is a tree of life.

—Proverbs 13:12

1258. God holds the whole world in His hands, and He already has a divine plan. Yet, He leaves room in His plan for us to make decisions and choices and to stretch our faith. We are made in the image and likeness of God. We are made to live by faith. God is only fully pleased when we live by faith.

And God said, Let us make man in our image, after our likeness: and let them have dominion over the fish of the sea, and over the fowl of the air, and over the cattle, and over all the earth, and over every creeping thing that creepeth upon the earth. So God created man in his own image, in the image of God created he him; male and female created he them. And God blessed them, and God said unto them, Be fruitful, and multiply, and replenish the earth, and subdue it: and have dominion over the fish of the sea, and over the fowl of the air, and over every living thing that moveth upon the earth.

—Genesis 1:26–28

Thou shalt also decree a thing, and it shall be established unto thee: and the light shall shine upon thy ways.

—Job 22:28

Where the Word of a king is, there is power: and who may say unto him, What doest thou?

—Ecclesiastes 8:4

And the Lord answered me, and said, Write the vision, and make it plain upon tables, that he may run that readeth it. For the vision is yet for an appointed time, but at the end it shall speak, and not lie: though it tarry, wait for it; because it will surely come, it will not tarry. Behold, his soul which is lifted up is not upright in him: but the just shall live by his faith.

—Habakkuk 2:2–4

1259. You're free when you no longer have to adjust yourself to be accepted by others. Rather, others have to accept you as you are. Like old people, who are old enough to stop having to pretend in order to *fit-in*. They really don't care. You have to accept them as they are. They've earned that. You have too. It's called personhood!

And he came to Nazareth, where he had been brought up: and, as his custom was, he went into the synagogue on the sabbath day, and stood up for to read. And there was delivered unto him the book of the prophet Esaias. And when he had opened the book, he found the place where it was written, The Spirit of the Lord is upon me, because he hath anointed me to

preach the gospel to the poor; he hath sent me to heal the brokenhearted, to preach deliverance to the captives, and recovering of sight to the blind, to set at liberty them that are bruised, To preach the acceptable year of the Lord. And he closed the book, and he gave it again to the minister, and sat down. And the eyes of all them that were in the synagogue were fastened on him. And he began to say unto them, This day is this scripture fulfilled in your ears. And all bare him witness, and wondered at the gracious words which proceeded out of his mouth. And they said, Is not this Joseph's son?

—Luke 4:16–22

1260. Just like the sky is bright and blue, and the sun is brilliant and shining, and the trees are green and brilliant; may your personality also be life-filled, brilliant, and vibrant! May you have the best that life yields, and may you enjoy life to the full!

But his delight is in the law of the Lord; and in his law doth he meditate day and night. And he shall be like a tree planted by the rivers of water, that bringeth forth his fruit in his season; his leaf also shall not wither; and whatsoever he doeth shall prosper.

—Psalm 1:2–3

1261. Regarding success, while you are believing for a miraculous anomaly, be sure to be practicing universal principles, which have a proven track record of results.

But rather seek ye the kingdom of God; and all these things shall be added unto you. Fear not, little flock; for it is your Father's good pleasure to give you the kingdom. Sell that ye have, and give alms; provide yourselves bags which wax not old, a treasure in the heavens that faileth not, where no thief approacheth, neither moth corrupteth. For where your treasure is, there will your heart be also.

—Luke 12:31-34

1262. Always think *problem prevention*, because problems always can happen.

Watch and pray, that ye enter not into temptation: the spirit indeed is willing, but the flesh is weak.

—Matthew 26:41

1263. After so many delays and denials, it can leave a heart cynical or suspicious of the possibility of a *"yes"*. Yet, if you have put your trust and reliance upon the promises of God's Word, and you are fulfilling the necessary steps of His principles, you can enthusiastically expect a fulfillment of His every promise with an eventual *"yes" and "amen!"*

For all the promises of God in him are yea, and in him Amen, unto the glory of God by us.

−2 Corinthians 1:20

To subvert a man in his cause, the Lord approveth not. Who is he that saith, and it cometh to pass, when the Lord

commandeth it not? Out of the mouth of the most High proceedeth not evil and good?

—Lamentations 3:36–38

1264. When does God, the Creator of life, the Most High Judge, say we have the constitutional right of *life, liberty, and the pursuit of happiness*? Even before conception. You existed in Him before conception. Therefore, when you and I were granted the right of being conceived, we also gained the right to live!

Then the Word of the Lord came unto me, saying, Before I formed thee in the belly I knew thee; and before thou camest forth out of the womb I sanctified thee, and I ordained thee a prophet unto the nations.

—Jeremiah 1:4–5

I will praise thee; for I am fearfully and wonderfully made: marvellous are thy works; and that my soul knoweth right well. My substance was not hid from thee, when I was made in secret, and curiously wrought in the lowest parts of the earth. Thine eyes did see my substance, yet being unperfect; and in thy book all my members were written, which in continuance were fashioned, when as yet there was none of them. How precious also are thy thoughts unto me, O God! how great is the sum of them! If I should count them, they are more in number than the sand: when I awake, I am still with thee.

—Psalm 139:14–18

1265. The purpose of being conscious of time and being aware of the years we have left, is not so we will be always thinking about the inevitability of the end. Rather, it is that we will live everyday focused on applying our heart, time, and energy upon fulfilling God's purpose for our years, no matter how many may remain.

So teach us to number our days, that we may apply our hearts unto wisdom.

—Psalm 90:12

1266. When God's mission becomes your mission, you're in submission, and you will then gain the victory.

Submit yourselves therefore to God. Resist the devil, and he will flee from you.

—James 4:7

1267. If you want to do your best, you've got to get your rest. If you make rest a priority, you will make the rest a priority.

And he said unto them, Come ye yourselves apart into a desert place, and rest a while: for there were many coming and going, and they had no leisure so much as to eat.

—Mark 6:31

1268. When faced with overwhelming circumstances, that seem to suck the air out of your lungs, pray anyway. Your prayers, even if they are short and painful to utter, are the *seeds* for your change, breakthrough, and wisdom to address your situation. God hears prayers. Even if they are short and low in volume, requiring painful effort to utter.

The righteous cry, and the Lord heareth, and delivereth them out of all their troubles.

—Psalm 34:17

1269. You have to know when to rest. You can't just keep going and going, and burning and burning. Even God tells the Sun to go down and rest a while, and let the Moon take over for a while.

And God made two great lights; the greater light to rule the day, and the lesser light to rule the night: he made the stars also.

—Genesis 1:16

1270. Success requires continual steps in the right direction.

The steps of a good man are ordered by the Lord: and he delighteth in his way.

—Psalm 37:23

1271. How you see yourself will determine where you will ultimately see yourself. If you see yourself as a successful, prosperous person, you will eventually manifest into what you see. See it. Then, be it. You've got the power!

Seest thou a man diligent in his business? he shall stand before kings; he shall not stand before mean men.

—Proverbs 22:29

1272. Eat at home. It's good for your health and it's good for your heart. Home is where the heart is!

Better is a dinner of herbs where love is, than a stalled ox and hatred therewith.

—Proverbs 15:17

1273. Minister your dose of The Holy Ghost daily to those who need your anointing! Don't waste your space of grace to taste the grapes of The Promised Land of God's goodness. Enjoy the best of success by following God's principles and laws of love!

And it shall come to pass, if thou shalt hearken diligently unto the voice of the Lord thy God, to observe and to do all his commandments which I command thee this day, that the Lord thy God will set thee on high above all nations of the earth: And all these blessings shall come on thee, and overtake thee, if thou shalt hearken unto the voice of the Lord thy God. Blessed shalt thou be in the city, and blessed shalt thou be in

the field. Blessed shall be the fruit of thy body, and the fruit of thy ground, and the fruit of thy cattle, the increase of thy kine, and the flocks of thy sheep. Blessed shall be thy basket and thy store. Blessed shalt thou be when thou comest in, and blessed shalt thou be when thou goest out. The Lord shall cause thine enemies that rise up against thee to be smitten before thy face: they shall come out against thee one way, and flee before thee seven ways. The Lord shall command the blessing upon thee in thy storehouses, and in all that thou settest thine hand unto; and he shall bless thee in the land which the Lord thy God giveth thee. The Lord shall establish thee an holy people unto himself, as he hath sworn unto thee, if thou shalt keep the commandments of the Lord thy God, and walk in his ways. And all people of the earth shall see that thou art called by the name of the Lord; and they shall be afraid of thee. And the Lord shall make thee plenteous in goods, in the fruit of thy body, and in the fruit of thy cattle, and in the fruit of thy ground, in the land which the Lord sware unto thy fathers to give thee. The Lord shall open unto thee his good treasure, the heaven to give the rain unto thy land in his season, and to bless all the work of thine hand: and thou shalt lend unto many nations, and thou shalt not borrow. And the Lord shall make thee the head, and not the tail; and thou shalt be above only, and thou shalt not be beneath; if that thou hearken unto the commandments of the Lord thy God, which I command thee this day, to observe and to do them: And thou shalt not go aside from any of the Words which I command thee this day, to the right hand, or to the left, to go after other gods to serve them.

—Deuteronomy 28:1–14

1274. In the face of the darkness in the land, God's love continues to shine in and through the lives of those who know Him best. May you rest in His care, safety, and shelter in this season!

And such as do wickedly against the covenant shall he corrupt by flatteries: but the people that do know their God shall be strong, and do exploits.

—Daniel 11:32

1275. You're welcome to enter into God's world of love, peace, joy, and hope by believing on the name of The Lord Jesus Christ. Accept Him by faith. Say, "Jesus, come into my heart. I believe You are The Son of God. I believe you died on the cross to pay for my sins. I believe God raised You from the dead for my forgiveness. I accept forgiveness. I accept you as my Lord and Savior. Thank You Jesus. Amen."

For God so loved the world, that he gave his only begotten Son, that whosoever believeth in him should not perish, but have everlasting life. For God sent not his Son into the world to condemn the world; but that the world through him might be saved. He that believeth on him is not condemned: but he that believeth not is condemned already, because he hath not believed in the name of the only begotten Son of God. And this is the condemnation, that light is come into the world, and men loved darkness rather than light, because their deeds were evil. For every one that doeth evil hateth the light, neither cometh to the light, lest his deeds should be reproved.

But he that doeth truth cometh to the light, that his deeds may be made manifest, that they are wrought in God.

—John 3:16–21

But what saith it? The Word is nigh thee, even in thy mouth, and in thy heart: that is, the Word of faith, which we preach; that if thou shalt confess with thy mouth the Lord Jesus, and shalt believe in thine heart that God hath raised him from the dead, thou shalt be saved. For with the heart man believeth unto righteousness; and with the mouth confession is made unto salvation. For the scripture saith, Whosoever believeth on him shall not be ashamed. For there is no difference between the Jew and the Greek: for the same Lord over all is rich unto all that call upon him. For whosoever shall call upon the name of the Lord shall be saved.

—Romans 10:8–13

1276. Do not accept the peril of the times, without choosing to make a difference. The times do not determine the outcome of the future. People do. And you and I are the ones to choose.

This know also, that in the last days perilous times shall come. For men shall be lovers of their own selves, covetous, boasters, proud, blasphemers, disobedient to parents, unthankful, unholy, Without natural affection, trucebreakers, false accusers, incontinent, fierce, despisers of those that are good, Traitors, heady, highminded, lovers of pleasures more

than lovers of God; Having a form of godliness, but denying the power thereof: from such turn away.

—2 Timothy 3:1–5

Run ye to and fro through the streets of Jerusalem, and see now, and know, and seek in the broad places thereof, if ye can find a man, if there be any that executeth judgment, that seeketh the truth; and I will pardon it.

—Jeremiah 5:1

1277. Succeeding is your rent for being in the earth!

The ransom of a man's life are his riches: but the poor heareth not rebuke.

—Proverbs 13:8

1278. You're halfway through your day! God has grace for you to go all the way! Be a champion! Fight all the way through. You can't lose! Because God is with you! God is for you! And God is in you! Greater is He that is in you, than he that is in the world!

Thy shoes shall be iron and brass; and as thy days, so shall thy strength be.

—Deuteronomy 33:25

1279. Stop complaining, and pray. Reign. Don't whine. Reign as royalty in your life. Take authority in prayer, and stop whining!

Thou shalt also decree a thing, and it shall be established unto thee: and the light shall shine upon thy ways.

—Job 22:28

1280. In the midst of all of life's high intensity circumstances, it's good to have the occasional *"decaf moment"*–the kind that doesn't add to the drama!

Thou wilt keep him in perfect peace, whose mind is stayed on thee: because he trusteth in thee. Trust ye in the Lord for ever: for in the Lord JEHOVAH is everlasting strength.

—Isaiah 26:3–4

1281. Don't worry. Pray. Prayer travels.

And when thou prayest, thou shalt not be as the hypocrites are: for they love to pray standing in the synagogues and in the corners of the streets, that they may be seen of men. Verily I say unto you, They have their reward. But thou, when thou prayest, enter into thy closet, and when thou hast shut thy door, pray to thy Father which is in secret; and thy Father which seeth in secret shall reward thee openly.

—Matthew 6:5–6

1282. Some say we are in the time of the end because of the severity of the times. The stakes seem higher. The threats seem more imposing and eminent. Yet, varying degrees of the enemy's attacks have always only released even greater measures of God's subduing power! Don't be afraid! Don't doubt! God's got this!

Moreover the law entered, that the offence might abound. But where sin abounded, grace did much more abound.

—Romans 5:20

1283. Our death is imminent, and we have no time to waste!

Whatsoever thy hand findeth to do, do it with thy might; for there is no work, nor device, nor knowledge, nor wisdom, in the grave, whither thou goest.

—Ecclesiastes 9:10

1284. Without focus there is no success.

Keep thy heart with all diligence; for out of it are the issues of life. Put away from thee a froward mouth, and perverse lips put far from thee. Let thine eyes look right on, and let thine eyelids look straight before thee. Ponder the path of thy feet, and let all thy ways be established. Turn not to the right hand nor to the left: remove thy foot from evil.

—Proverbs 4:23–27

1285. Life can be overwhelming sometimes. When you can't handle it, leave it in the hands of The Lord.

Rejoice in the Lord always: and again I say, Rejoice. Let your moderation be known unto all men. The Lord is at hand. Be careful for nothing; but in every thing by prayer and supplication with thanksgiving let your requests be made known unto God. And the peace of God, which passeth all understanding, shall keep your hearts and minds through Christ Jesus. Finally, brethren, whatsoever things are true, whatsoever things are honest, whatsoever things are just, whatsoever things are pure, whatsoever things are lovely, whatsoever things are of good report; if there be any virtue, and if there be any praise, think on these things. Those things, which ye have both learned, and received, and heard, and seen in me, do: and the God of peace shall be with you.

—Philippians 4:4–9

1286. We must play the hand we've been dealt, and try to make our best move that could possibly turn this nation back to morality. Otherwise, the continued moral declines will lead the nation into a further abysmal free–fall into the clutches of Hell! We may not have all *aces*, but we do want to avoid giving the devil the opportunity of winning a straight flush, ending in us losing the whole pot!

The lot is cast into the lap; but the whole disposing thereof is of the Lord.

—Proverbs 16:33

1287. Riches are facilitated through time, talent, and resources. Riches are guaranteed through passion, perseverance, and determination.

In all labour there is profit: but the talk of the lips tendeth only to penury.

—Proverbs 14:23

The crown of the wise is their riches: but the foolishness of fools is folly.

—Proverbs 14:24

For a dream cometh through the multitude of business; and a fool's voice is known by multitude of words.

—Ecclesiastes 5:3

In the morning sow thy seed, and in the evening withhold not thine hand: for thou knowest not whether shall prosper, either this or that, or whether they both shall be alike good.

—Ecclesiastes 11:6

1288. Stop saying and start praying!

If my people, which are called by my name, shall humble themselves, and pray, and seek my face, and turn from their wicked ways; then will I hear from heaven, and will forgive their sin, and will heal their land.

—2 Chronicles 7:14

1289. The Lord is working on our behalf! And we're blessed! Blessed! Blessed! Oh! So, blessed! Leave it in God's hands. He sees the big picture and the long-term victory!

And we know that all things work together for good to them that love God, to them who are the called according to his purpose.

—Romans 8:28

1290. Be still and trust God with your life's journey. God wouldn't stop the train tracks short of the trip. He started you on the journey. He will make sure you finish the trip.

Being confident of this very thing, that he which hath begun a good work in you will perform it until the day of Jesus Christ:

—Philippians 1:6

1291. Regarding television, there's few things on that's worth our time, worth our dime, or worth our minds! Spend time making the most of your energy by being productive, making the most of your money by investing in lasting things like knowledge and wisdom, and making the most of your mind by actually reading, studying, and getting better at what you do for a living.

Whatsoever thy hand findeth to do, do it with thy might; for there is no work, nor device, nor knowledge, nor wisdom, in the grave, whither thou goest.

—Ecclesiastes 9:10

1292. If you were able to take a hot bath, in a warm home this morning, get food from the fridge, drink clean water, turn on the T.V. or look on your cellphone, then, be thankful for *daily living*. You're blessed more than many!

Blessed be the Lord, who daily loadeth us with benefits, even the God of our salvation. Selah.

—Psalm 68:19

1293. Mankind at his or her best state is but a vain show. No matter how proud and confident one may appear, he or she still has problems, bills, health challenges, family problems, doubts, fears, etc.; to try to overcome. We all need the same thing: love, understanding, and Jesus.

Surely every man walketh in a vain shew: surely they are disquieted in vain: he heapeth up riches, and knoweth not who shall gather them. And now, Lord, what wait I for? my hope is in thee.

—Psalm 39:6–7

1294. What comes after the prophetic utterances of Jeremiah in The Bible is Lamentations for those who failed to heed his first utterances. This same pattern will repeat itself in America if we do not heed the voice of God's Word as the guide for voting in the elections.

If thou wilt return, O Israel, saith the Lord, return unto me: and if thou wilt put away thine abominations out of my sight, then shalt thou not remove. And thou shalt swear, The Lord liveth, in truth, in judgment, and in righteousness; and the nations shall bless themselves in him, and in him shall they glory. For thus saith the Lord to the men of Judah and Jerusalem, Break up your fallow ground, and sow not among thorns. Circumcise yourselves to the Lord, and take away the foreskins of your heart, ye men of Judah and inhabitants of Jerusalem: lest my fury come forth like fire, and burn that none can quench it, because of the evil of your doings.

—Jeremiah 4:1–4

How doth the city sit solitary, that was full of people! how is she become as a widow! she that was great among the nations, and princess among the provinces, how is she become tributary! She weepeth sore in the night, and her tears are on her cheeks: among all her lovers she hath none to comfort her: all her friends have dealt treacherously with her, they are become her enemies. Judah is gone into captivity because of affliction, and because of great servitude: she dwelleth among the heathen, she findeth no rest: all her persecutors overtook her between the straits. The ways of Zion do mourn, because none come to the solemn feasts: all her gates are desolate: her priests sigh, her virgins are afflicted, and she is in bitterness. Her adversaries are the chief, her enemies prosper; for the Lord hath afflicted her for the multitude of her transgressions: her children are gone into captivity before the enemy. And from the daughter of Zion all her beauty is departed: her

princes are become like harts that find no pasture, and they are gone without strength before the pursuer.

—Lamentations 1:1–6

1295. An idea is one thing, but action is everything.

Even so faith, if it hath not works, is dead, being alone. Yea, a man may say, Thou hast faith, and I have works: shew me thy faith without thy works, and I will shew thee my faith by my works.

—James 2:17–18

1296. Education is valuable. The only people who talk disparagingly about academics are people who lack education.

Buy the truth, and sell it not; also wisdom, and instruction, and understanding.

—Proverbs 23:23

1297. Evaluate The Bible. Evaluate your heart. Evaluate the issues. Evaluate your morals. Then, make a decision most closely aligned, and take action.

Be of good courage, and let us play the men for our people, and for the cities of our God: and the Lord do that which seemeth him good.

—2 Samuel 10:12

1298. Most religious people don't think or they are afraid to think, because thinking often causes us to challenge our beliefs, which can be scary, because of uncertainty. However, we walk by faith and not by sight. If that wasn't so, we never would have made it to the Moon, flown the first airplane, or explored the excavation that discovered The Dead Sea Scrolls!

And I will give thee the treasures of darkness, and hidden riches of secret places, that thou mayest know that I, the Lord, which call thee by thy name, am the God of Israel.

—Isaiah 45:3

1299. Class costs, but the resulting excellency is worth the investment.

Now it came to pass in the days of Ahasuerus, (this is Ahasuerus which reigned, from India even unto Ethiopia, over an hundred and seven and twenty provinces:) That in those days, when the king Ahasuerus sat on the throne of his kingdom, which was in Shushan the palace, In the third year of his reign, he made a feast unto all his princes and his servants; the power of Persia and Media, the nobles and princes of the provinces, being before him: When he shewed the riches of his glorious kingdom and the honour of his excellent majesty many days, even an hundred and fourscore days. And when these days were expired, the king made a feast unto all the people that were present in Shushan the palace, both unto great and small, seven days, in the court of the garden of the king's palace; Where were white, green, and

blue, hangings, fastened with cords of fine linen and purple to silver rings and pillars of marble: the beds were of gold and silver, upon a pavement of red, and blue, and white, and black, marble. And they gave them drink in vessels of gold, (the vessels being diverse one from another,) and royal wine in abundance, according to the state of the king. And the drinking was according to the law; none did compel: for so the king had appointed to all the officers of his house, that they should do according to every man's pleasure.

—Esther 1:1–8

1300. We're all getting older. No matter what your age may be life is fragile. May we all live with eternity in mind. Make the most of each hour, day, week, month, and year, and be ready to meet Jesus Christ, your Maker, when your life is over on this earth.

Boast not thyself of to morrow; for thou knowest not what a day may bring forth.

—Proverbs 27:1

1301. When a person is content within his or herself, he or she can focus more on being of service to others.

Take heed therefore unto yourselves, and to all the flock, over the which the Holy Ghost hath made you overseers, to feed the church of God, which he hath purchased with his own blood.

—Acts 20:28

Pastor Terrance Levise Turner, MBA

1302. The best time to repair the roof is when the Sun is shining. Take care of your problem while it's not a problem, and then you will be better able to prevent the recurrence of the problem.

The beginning of strife is as when one letteth out water: therefore leave off contention, before it be meddled with.

—Proverbs 17:14

1303. A royal seed will always rise to a place of ascendancy, no matter how deep it is buried beneath the soil of adversity. Like a mighty oak springing from the encasement of an acorn, greatness will rise to its preordained destiny!

And it came to pass in the morning that his spirit was troubled; and he sent and called for all the magicians of Egypt, and all the wise men thereof: and Pharaoh told them his dream; but there was none that could interpret them unto Pharaoh. Then spake the chief butler unto Pharaoh, saying, I do remember my faults this day: Pharaoh was wroth with his servants, and put me in ward in the captain of the guard's house, both me and the chief baker: And we dreamed a dream in one night, I and he; we dreamed each man according to the interpretation of his dream. And there was there with us a young man, an Hebrew, servant to the captain of the guard; and we told him, and he interpreted to us our dreams; to each man according to his dream he did interpret. And it came to pass, as he interpreted to us, so it was; me he restored unto mine office, and him he hanged. Then Pharaoh sent and called Joseph, and they brought him hastily out of the dungeon: and

he shaved himself, and changed his raiment, and came in unto Pharaoh. And Pharaoh said unto Joseph, I have dreamed a dream, and there is none that can interpret it: and I have heard say of thee, that thou canst understand a dream to interpret it. And Joseph answered Pharaoh, saying, It is not in me: God shall give Pharaoh an answer of peace. And Pharaoh said unto Joseph, In my dream, behold, I stood upon the bank of the river: And, behold, there came up out of the river seven kine, fatfleshed and well favoured; and they fed in a meadow: And, behold, seven other kine came up after them, poor and very ill favoured and leanfleshed, such as I never saw in all the land of Egypt for badness: And the lean and the ill favoured kine did eat up the first seven fat kine: And when they had eaten them up, it could not be known that they had eaten them; but they were still ill favoured, as at the beginning. So I awoke. And I saw in my dream, and, behold, seven ears came up in one stalk, full and good: And, behold, seven ears, withered, thin, and blasted with the east wind, sprung up after them: And the thin ears devoured the seven good ears: and I told this unto the magicians; but there was none that could declare it to me. And Joseph said unto Pharaoh, The dream of Pharaoh is one: God hath shewed Pharaoh what he is about to do. The seven good kine are seven years; and the seven good ears are seven years: the dream is one. And the seven thin and ill favoured kine that came up after them are seven years; and the seven empty ears blasted with the east wind shall be seven years of famine. This is the thing which I have spoken unto Pharaoh: What God is about to do he sheweth unto Pharaoh. Behold, there come seven years of great plenty throughout all the land of Egypt: And there shall arise after them seven years of famine; and all the plenty shall be forgotten in the land of

Egypt; and the famine shall consume the land; And the plenty shall not be known in the land by reason of that famine following; for it shall be very grievous. And for that the dream was doubled unto Pharaoh twice; it is because the thing is established by God, and God will shortly bring it to pass. Now therefore let Pharaoh look out a man discreet and wise, and set him over the land of Egypt. Let Pharaoh do this, and let him appoint officers over the land, and take up the fifth part of the land of Egypt in the seven plenteous years. And let them gather all the food of those good years that come, and lay up corn under the hand of Pharaoh, and let them keep food in the cities. And that food shall be for store to the land against the seven years of famine, which shall be in the land of Egypt; that the land perish not through the famine. And the thing was good in the eyes of Pharaoh, and in the eyes of all his servants. And Pharaoh said unto his servants, Can we find such a one as this is, a man in whom the Spirit of God is? And Pharaoh said unto Joseph, Forasmuch as God hath shewed thee all this, there is none so discreet and wise as thou art: Thou shalt be over my house, and according unto thy word shall all my people be ruled: only in the throne will I be greater than thou. And Pharaoh said unto Joseph, See, I have set thee over all the land of Egypt. And Pharaoh took off his ring from his hand, and put it upon Joseph's hand, and arrayed him in vestures of fine linen, and put a gold chain about his neck; And he made him to ride in the second chariot which he had; and they cried before him, Bow the knee: and he made him ruler over all the land of Egypt.

—Genesis 41:8–43

1304. If you want to know the will of God, read His Words in the Bible.

Seek ye out of the book of the Lord, and read: no one of these shall fail, none shall want her mate: for my mouth it hath commanded, and his spirit it hath gathered them.

—Isaiah 34:16

1305. You may not know where you are, but God knows where you are, and He has the plan.

Behold, I go forward, but he is not there; and backward, but I cannot perceive him: On the left hand, where he doth work, but I cannot behold him: he hideth himself on the right hand, that I cannot see him: But he knoweth the way that I take: when he hath tried me, I shall come forth as gold.

—Job 23:8–10

1306. Pray for the world in which we live.

I exhort therefore, that, first of all, supplications, prayers, intercessions, and giving of thanks, be made for all men; For kings, and for all that are in authority; that we may lead a quiet and peaceable life in all godliness and honesty.

–1 Timothy 2:1–2

1307. In regard to the presidency, it is not a man or woman thing. It is a right or wrong thing. It's about what's best and

what's right for the nation; for the health of the nation; for the health of our borders; for the health of our children; for the health of our families; for the health of our economy; for the defense of the Constitution; and for the health of our morals. It's not a man or woman thing. It's simply a right or wrong thing.

Be of good courage, and let us play the men for our people, and for the cities of our God: and the Lord do that which seemeth him good.

–2 Samuel 10:12

1308. Once you open the cage door of fear, and release yourself from all that has been restricting you, you will become bold as a lion! And the world will hear you roar!

The wicked flee when no man pursueth: but the righteous are bold as a lion.

—Proverbs 28:1

1309. Fear is like the wind, you can't see it. You just feel it. It is sent to keep you from obtaining your miracle. Don't Fear. It's only false evidence appearing real.

And straightway Jesus constrained his disciples to get into a ship, and to go before him unto the other side, while he sent the multitudes away. And when he had sent the multitudes away, he went up into a mountain apart to pray: and when the evening was come, he was there alone. But the ship was now

in the midst of the sea, tossed with waves: for the wind was contrary. And in the fourth watch of the night Jesus went unto them, walking on the sea. And when the disciples saw him walking on the sea, they were troubled, saying, It is a spirit; and they cried out for fear. But straightway Jesus spake unto them, saying, Be of good cheer; it is I; be not afraid. And Peter answered him and said, Lord, if it be thou, bid me come unto thee on the water. And he said, Come. And when Peter was come down out of the ship, he walked on the water, to go to Jesus. But when he saw the wind boisterous, he was afraid; and beginning to sink, he cried, saying, Lord, save me. And immediately Jesus stretched forth his hand, and caught him, and said unto him, O thou of little faith, wherefore didst thou doubt? And when they were come into the ship, the wind ceased. Then they that were in the ship came and worshipped him, saying, Of a truth thou art the Son of God.

—Matthew 14:22–33

1310. If you fought the fight that needed to be fought, you've won. It doesn't matter if your nose is bleeding, your lip is swollen, and your eyes are black. If the fight was necessary, and you boldly answered the call, you have won. Some spoils are worth the fight to obtain them!

Know ye not that they which run in a race run all, but one receiveth the prize? So run, that ye may obtain. And every man that striveth for the mastery is temperate in all things. Now they do it to obtain a corruptible crown; but we an incorruptible. I therefore so run, not as uncertainly; so fight I, not as one that beateth the air: But I keep under my body, and

bring it into subjection: lest that by any means, when I have preached to others, I myself should be a castaway.

–1 Corinthians 9:24–27

Fight the good fight of faith, lay hold on eternal life, whereunto thou art also called, and hast professed a good profession before many witnesses.

–1 Timothy 6:12

1311. Is not a bird in a cage still a bird? Though restricted from manifesting its natural–born wonder? Never doubt your natural–born gifts, talents, and calling due to temporary restrictions, hinderances, or delays. Keep on singing! Your liberation is coming soon!

For the gifts and calling of God are without repentance.

—Romans 11:29

1312. God has given you time, and He has given you a mind. Now you must decide to make that dime!

Whatsoever thy hand findeth to do, do it with thy might; for there is no work, nor device, nor knowledge, nor wisdom, in the grave, whither thou goest.

—Ecclesiastes 9:10

1313. To totally please God, we must actively pursue righteousness. Jesus made us righteous, through His precious

blood. However, we must actively pursue righteousness, in order to fulfill the joy of The Father's expectation when He gave His Son. We won't achieve perfection. Yet, we must actively walk after the spirit, and not after the flesh.

There is therefore now no condemnation to them which are in Christ Jesus, who walk not after the flesh, but after the Spirit. For the law of the Spirit of life in Christ Jesus hath made me free from the law of sin and death. For what the law could not do, in that it was weak through the flesh, God sending his own Son in the likeness of sinful flesh, and for sin, condemned sin in the flesh: that the righteousness of the law might be fulfilled in us, who walk not after the flesh, but after the Spirit.

—Romans 8:1–4

1314. Love is, if it is: and it ain't, if it ain't. Actions tell the difference.

Yea, a man may say, Thou hast faith, and I have works: shew me thy faith without thy works, and I will shew thee my faith by my works.

—James 2:18

1315. Achieving God's will is the source of eternal strength and energy. It helps you to endure the common challenges of life, and gives you supernatural ability to overcome.

Jesus saith unto them, My meat is to do the will of him that sent me, and to finish his work.

—John 4:34

1316. Tomorrow will be better.

Take therefore no thought for the morrow: for the morrow shall take thought for the things of itself. Sufficient unto the day is the evil thereof.

—Matthew 6:34

1317. The Lord is your strength and shield. He is the lifter of your head. He will never fail you. He will help you endure. He is your Rock.

The Lord is my strength and my shield; my heart trusted in him, and I am helped: therefore my heart greatly rejoiceth; and with my song will I praise him. The Lord is their strength, and he is the saving strength of his anointed. Save thy people, and bless thine inheritance: feed them also, and lift them up for ever.

—Psalm 28:7–9

1318. Expand your vision and expectation beyond your current circumstances to see something more favorable for your future. God is so much bigger, and so much better than what you've ever experienced!

If they obey and serve him, they shall spend their days in prosperity, and their years in pleasures.

—Job 36:11

1319. If God be for you, who can be against you? If God says you're blessed, who can curse you? If God told you to do it, then, who can stop you? God doesn't change His mind in blessing you! He loves you!

To subvert a man in his cause, the Lord approveth not. Who is he that saith, and it cometh to pass, when the Lord commandeth it not? Out of the mouth of the most High proceedeth not evil and good?

—Lamentations 3:36–38

1320. Take time to fill your heart with the truth of God's Word. Feelings and emotional states are temporary. Yet, the anointing of God's Word is eternal. It destroys the yoke and removes the heavy burden off of your life.

Then shall the kingdom of heaven be likened unto ten virgins, which took their lamps, and went forth to meet the bridegroom. And five of them were wise, and five were foolish. They that were foolish took their lamps, and took no oil with them: but the wise took oil in their vessels with their lamps. While the bridegroom tarried, they all slumbered and slept. And at midnight there was a cry made, Behold, the bridegroom cometh; go ye out to meet him. Then all those virgins arose, and trimmed their lamps. And the foolish said unto the wise, Give us of your oil; for our lamps are gone out. But the wise answered, saying, Not so; lest there be not enough for us and you: but go ye rather to them that sell, and

buy for yourselves. And while they went to buy, the bridegroom came; and they that were ready went in with him to the marriage: and the door was shut. Afterward came also the other virgins, saying, Lord, Lord, open to us. But he answered and said, Verily I say unto you, I know you not. Watch therefore, for ye know neither the day nor the hour wherein the Son of man cometh.

—Matthew 25:1–13

1321. Your mountain of opposition contains the treasures to enrich your life forever. If you remove it by faith, you will discover that nothing will be impossible to you!

And Jesus said unto them, Because of your unbelief: for verily I say unto you, If ye have faith as a grain of mustard seed, ye shall say unto this mountain, Remove hence to yonder place; and it shall remove; and nothing shall be impossible unto you. Howbeit this kind goeth not out but by prayer and fasting.

—Matthew 17:20–21

1322. A praising woman is like spinach to *Popeye*. She builds a man up. A fussing woman is like *kryptonite* to a Super-man. Whether it's his mother, sister, aunt, or wife; or the cheerleaders on the sidelines. As the hero continues to do exploits, he will receive more praise!

Let them shout for joy, and be glad, that favour my righteous cause: yea, let them say continually, Let the Lord be

magnified, which hath pleasure in the prosperity of his servant.

—Psalm 35:27

1323. Every wife should treat her husband as if he was the President of the United States. Every husband should treat his wife as if she was the First Lady. All parents should treat their children as if they were the First Family. Respect, love, and honor are the keys.

Wives, submit yourselves unto your own husbands, as unto the Lord. For the husband is the head of the wife, even as Christ is the head of the church: and he is the saviour of the body. Therefore as the church is subject unto Christ, so let the wives be to their own husbands in every thing. Husbands, love your wives, even as Christ also loved the church, and gave himself for it; That he might sanctify and cleanse it with the washing of water by the Word, That he might present it to himself a glorious church, not having spot, or wrinkle, or any such thing; but that it should be holy and without blemish. So ought men to love their wives as their own bodies. He that loveth his wife loveth himself. For no man ever yet hated his own flesh; but nourisheth and cherisheth it, even as the Lord the church: For we are members of his body, of his flesh, and of his bones. For this cause shall a man leave his father and mother, and shall be joined unto his wife, and they two shall be one flesh. This is a great mystery: but I speak concerning Christ and the church. Nevertheless let every one of you in particular so love his wife even as himself; and the wife see that she reverence her husband.

—Ephesians 5:22–33

Children, obey your parents in the Lord: for this is right. Honour thy father and mother; which is the first commandment with promise; That it may be well with thee, and thou mayest live long on the earth. And, ye fathers, provoke not your children to wrath: but bring them up in the nurture and admonition of the Lord.

—Ephesians 6:1–4

1324. Anytime you have the opportunity to be outstanding, you might as well take it! You only live once. You might as well make a splash!

Seest thou a man diligent in his business? he shall stand before kings; he shall not stand before mean men.

—Proverbs 22:29

1325. The accomplishment of great deeds requires great confidence. Great confidence is obtained through the acknowledgement of the greatness, which God put in you.

That the communication of thy faith may become effectual by the acknowledging of every good thing which is in you in Christ Jesus.

—Philemon 6

1326. Create the vision of your future with your words and actions. Sow the right works and words, and you will receive your harvest. Stay motivated and diligent. You will be rewarded.

A man shall be satisfied with good by the fruit of his mouth: and the recompence of a man's hands shall be rendered unto him.

—Proverbs 12:14

1327. Often what seems to be "the end of the world!" is only a part of being in the world. You can handle it!

There hath no temptation taken you but such as is common to man: but God is faithful, who will not suffer you to be tempted above that ye are able; but will with the temptation also make a way to escape, that ye may be able to bear it.

–1 Corinthians 10:13

1328. No matter what you've lost or what pain you've suffered or what delays you've had, God can and will restore you better than you were before.

And I will restore to you the years that the locust hath eaten, the cankerworm, and the caterpiller, and the palmerworm, my great army which I sent among you.

—Joel 2:25

1329. God already wishes above everything, that we *"prosper, and be in health; even as our soul prospers"*. If we will do what's necessary to obtain the blessings, we will fulfill His desire. And the blessing of The Lord makes rich, and He adds no sorrow with it!

Beloved, I wish above all things that thou mayest prosper and be in health, even as thy soul prospereth.

–3 John 1:2

The blessing of the Lord, it maketh rich, and he addeth no sorrow with it.

—Proverbs 10:22

1330. We must live our remaining days on purpose. We must evaluate where we are, and maximize our remaining strength to make the most of our remaining life and influence on Earth.

For to him that is joined to all the living there is hope: for a living dog is better than a dead lion. For the living know that they shall die: but the dead know not any thing, neither have they any more a reward; for the memory of them is forgotten. Also their love, and their hatred, and their envy, is now perished; neither have they any more a portion for ever in any thing that is done under the sun. Go thy way, eat thy bread with joy, and drink thy wine with a merry heart; for God now accepteth thy works. Let thy garments be always white; and let thy head lack no ointment. Live joyfully with the wife

whom thou lovest all the days of the life of thy vanity, which he hath given thee under the sun, all the days of thy vanity: for that is thy portion in this life, and in thy labour which thou takest under the sun. Whatsoever thy hand findeth to do, do it with thy might; for there is no work, nor device, nor knowledge, nor wisdom, in the grave, whither thou goest. I returned, and saw under the sun, that the race is not to the swift, nor the battle to the strong, neither yet bread to the wise, nor yet riches to men of understanding, nor yet favour to men of skill; but time and chance happeneth to them all.

—Ecclesiastes 9:4–11

1331. Do not be discouraged. If you have started to seek The Lord and to do His will, He has heard you and He has taken notice. Your blessing, answer, and help are on the way!

Then said he unto me, Fear not, Daniel: for from the first day that thou didst set thine heart to understand, and to chasten thyself before thy God, thy words were heard, and I am come for thy words.

—Daniel 10:12

And this is the confidence that we have in him, that, if we ask any thing according to his will, he heareth us: and if we know that he hear us, whatsoever we ask, we know that we have the petitions that we desired of him.

–1 John 5:14–15

1332. Don't let anyone define your faith for you. They can influence your faith, but don't let them define it. Your faith-walk is between you and God. If God is pleased with you, what can man add to you? Keep passionately moving in the direction of faith. You will never be late.

We having the same spirit of faith, according as it is written, I believed, and therefore have I spoken; we also believe, and therefore speak;

–2 Corinthians 4:13

1333. Results come from hard, smart work. If you do what successful people do, you can have what successful people have.

Then Peter opened his mouth, and said, Of a truth I perceive that God is no respecter of persons: But in every nation he that feareth him, and worketh righteousness, is accepted with him.

—Acts 10:34–35

1334. You have to be determined to make money first, in order to have enough to help others. The greatest way to please God is to use your time, talents, and resources to help others. However, you first have to discover your treasure, before it can become valuable to others.

But rather seek ye the kingdom of God; and all these things shall be added unto you. Fear not, little flock; for it is your

Father's good pleasure to give you the kingdom. Sell that ye have, and give alms; provide yourselves bags which wax not old, a treasure in the heavens that faileth not, where no thief approacheth, neither moth corrupteth. For where your treasure is, there will your heart be also.

—Luke 12:31–34

1335. Success is a matter of time, effort, and favor. It is God's will that you succeed in life. As you put forth the necessary efforts, over time, you will increase in favor. Success is necessary, and it is God's perfect will for your life.

A feast is made for laughter, and wine maketh merry: but money answereth all things.

—Ecclesiastes 10:19

1336. It is our job to discover our gifts and talents in life, and then refine them. We are responsible for extracting the value out of what God has invested in us. We must recognize that we are valuable. Then, we must work diligently to maximize that value. That's our responsibility and gift back to ourselves, our family, society, and ultimately, to God.

The slothful man roasteth not that which he took in hunting: but the substance of a diligent man is precious.

—Proverbs 12:27

1337. Principles, or the lack thereof, determine how you make up your mind.

I call heaven and earth to record this day against you, that I have set before you life and death, blessing and cursing: therefore choose life, that both thou and thy seed may live.

—Deuteronomy 30:19

Multitudes, multitudes in the valley of decision: for the day of the Lord is near in the valley of decision.

—Joel 3:14

1338. Your brain is prime real estate. Don't corrupt the resources. Be careful of what you allow to be sown into the ground, or and what you allow to be built on it. Avoid useless material, information, endeavors, or relationships. You are sitting on a gold mine! Don't corrupt your resources.

He that tilleth his land shall have plenty of bread: but he that followeth after vain persons shall have poverty enough.

—Proverbs 28:19

1339. When the strings are detached, you have the license to ascend higher.

Is not this the fast that I have chosen? to loose the bands of wickedness, to undo the heavy burdens, and to let the oppressed go free, and that ye break every yoke?

—Isaiah 58:6

But they that wait upon the Lord shall renew their strength; they shall mount up with wings as eagles; they shall run, and not be weary; and they shall walk, and not faint.

—Isaiah 40:31

1340. Obey the Lord, and leave the outcome to Him.

Be of good courage, and let us play the men for our people, and for the cities of our God: and the Lord do that which seemeth him good.

—2 Samuel 10:12

1341. A mighty nation with corrupt morals is like a mighty giant with bone disease. No matter how great its outward appearance or exploits, eventually it will collapse, due to the weakened foundations. Only through repentance and returning to morals will the mighty giant continue to stand. Pray for our nation.

If the foundations be destroyed, what can the righteous do?

—Psalm 11:3

The wicked shall be turned into hell, and all the nations that forget God.

—Psalm 9:17

Pastor Terrance Levise Turner, MBA

When the righteous are in authority, the people rejoice: but when the wicked beareth rule, the people mourn.

—Proverbs 29:2

If my people, which are called by my name, shall humble themselves, and pray, and seek my face, and turn from their wicked ways; then will I hear from heaven, and will forgive their sin, and will heal their land.

–2 Chronicles 7:14

1342. May the Lord always protect the integrity of our marriages. May love and commitment bind our hearts together, and may nothing violate the covenant between one man and one woman, for a lifetime.

And Mizpah; for he said, The Lord watch between me and thee, when we are absent one from another. If thou shalt afflict my daughters, or if thou shalt take other wives beside my daughters, no man is with us; see, God is witness betwixt me and thee. And Laban said to Jacob, Behold this heap, and behold this pillar, which I have cast betwixt me and thee: This heap be witness, and this pillar be witness, that I will not pass over this heap to thee, and that thou shalt not pass over this heap and this pillar unto me, for harm. The God of Abraham, and the God of Nahor, the God of their father, judge betwixt us. And Jacob sware by the fear of his father Isaac. Then Jacob offered sacrifice upon the mount, and called his brethren to eat bread: and they did eat bread, and tarried all night in the mount.

—Genesis 31:49–54

1343. Don't be so idealistic that you are foolish. Neither, be so practical that you refuse to believe.

Then said Mary unto the angel, How shall this be, seeing I know not a man? And the angel answered and said unto her, The Holy Ghost shall come upon thee, and the power of the Highest shall overshadow thee: therefore also that holy thing which shall be born of thee shall be called the Son of God. And, behold, thy cousin Elisabeth, she hath also conceived a son in her old age: and this is the sixth month with her, who was called barren. For with God nothing shall be impossible. And Mary said, Behold the handmaid of the Lord; be it unto me according to thy word. And the angel departed from her.

—Luke 1:34–38

1344. The world is only now starting to reach a post-slavery period. Slavery is a state of mind. Or rather, *mind control*. The world is flat!

Not for that we have dominion over your faith, but are helpers of your joy: for by faith ye stand.

—2 Corinthians 1:24

1345. If you're first, you could never be last.

And over these three presidents; of whom Daniel was first: that the princes might give accounts unto them, and the king

should have no damage. Then this Daniel was preferred above the presidents and princes, because an excellent spirit was in him; and the king thought to set him over the whole realm. Then the presidents and princes sought to find occasion against Daniel concerning the kingdom; but they could find none occasion nor fault; forasmuch as he was faithful, neither was there any error or fault found in him.

—Daniel 6:2–4

1346. May you be guided in your every step today. Let God's principles that are found in the Bible be your guiding source. You will never regret following His principles, and you will be blessed with the outcome.

The steps of a good man are ordered by the Lord: and he delighteth in his way.

—Psalm 37:23

1347. The true principles of the Constitution of the United States should be upheld by all government officials. The principles were founded upon the Bible. The economy will be strengthened by allowing businesses to thrive and prosper without undue tax burdens. Prosperous businesses create new jobs. Prosperity in a nation is spear-headed by those who have learned how to prosper. Therefore, rather than, penalizing prosperity, and redistributing to those who hasn't earned it, freedom for all to prosper should be protected, not penalized.

When the righteous are in authority, the people rejoice: but when the wicked beareth rule, the people mourn.

—Proverbs 29:2

1348. The survival of this nation is based on a strong moral base, which relies upon the long-standing principles of the foundational documents this country was established on, which are the Bible and the Constitution. Only leaders that uphold those principles should be elected into government offices.

If the foundations be destroyed, what can the righteous do?

—Psalm 11:3

The wicked shall be turned into hell, and all the nations that forget God.

—Psalm 9:17

When the righteous are in authority, the people rejoice: but when the wicked beareth rule, the people mourn.

—Proverbs 29:2

I exhort therefore, that, first of all, supplications, prayers, intercessions, and giving of thanks, be made for all men; For kings, and for all that are in authority; that we may lead a quiet and peaceable life in all godliness and honesty.

−1 Timothy 2:1–2

Pastor Terrance Levise Turner, MBA

1349. Keep on praying! It's not over until The Statue of Liberty sings!

If my people, which are called by my name, shall humble themselves, and pray, and seek my face, and turn from their wicked ways; then will I hear from heaven, and will forgive their sin, and will heal their land.

–2 Chronicles 7:14

I exhort therefore, that, first of all, supplications, prayers, intercessions, and giving of thanks, be made for all men; For kings, and for all that are in authority; that we may lead a quiet and peaceable life in all godliness and honesty.

–1 Timothy 2:1–2

1350. You always have made it in between mountains. You can make it through this valley as well. There are treasures in the valleys as well as in the mountains. You must continue to dig. *Valley–time* is learning–time. Keep digging! Your next mountain is just ahead, and *there's gold in them there hills*! And, in the valleys!

Enlarge the place of thy tent, and let them stretch forth the curtains of thine habitations: spare not, lengthen thy cords, and strengthen thy stakes; For thou shalt break forth on the right hand and on the left; and thy seed shall inherit the Gentiles, and make the desolate cities to be inhabited.

—Isaiah 54:2–3

1351. You have been called to the kingdom for such a time as this. This is your time to fulfill your destiny. We all have a specific purpose that only we can do. If we are willing to prepare for it, and fight for it, God will help us to fulfill it.

For if thou altogether holdest thy peace at this time, then shall there enlargement and deliverance arise to the Jews from another place; but thou and thy father's house shall be destroyed: and who knoweth whether thou art come to the kingdom for such a time as this?

—Esther 4:14

1352. God is the God of miracles to deliver us, and ministry to sustain us. God is whatever you need, and He knows when, where, how, and why. God is God in our every situation and circumstance.

Behold, I am the Lord, the God of all flesh: is there any thing too hard for me?

—Jeremiah 32:27

1353. There's no failure in God. We can depend on Him. Call out to Him. He will answer your prayer. Jesus, He can fix it, whatever your problem may be. Call out to Him. He will fix it for you.

For whosoever shall call upon the name of the Lord shall be saved.

—Romans 10:13

1354. As you view and process all of the temporary issues that are in the world, be sure to save enough critical space on your mental hard-drive for solving life's *real* long-term problems. Don't worry!

A thousand shall fall at thy side, and ten thousand at thy right hand; but it shall not come nigh thee. Only with thine eyes shalt thou behold and see the reward of the wicked. Because thou hast made the Lord, which is my refuge, even the most High, thy habitation; There shall no evil befall thee, neither shall any plague come nigh thy dwelling.

—Psalm 91:7–10

1355. Light shines brightest and most contrastingly in the face of darkness. Let your light so very much shine before all men, in the midst of the confusion of transition. Let righteousness rule. Not our deeply seated opinions. Law and order is the will of God, regardless of personal opinions.

Ye are the salt of the earth: but if the salt have lost his savour, wherewith shall it be salted? it is thenceforth good for nothing, but to be cast out, and to be trodden under foot of men. Ye are the light of the world. A city that is set on an hill cannot be hid. Neither do men light a candle, and put it under a bushel, but on a candlestick; and it giveth light unto all that are in the house. Let your light so shine before men, that they may see your good works, and glorify your Father which is in heaven.

—Matthew 5:13–16

1356. Please consider that Jesus is the only answer to the challenges in the world today. Enter into His kingdom way of thinking and living. He will surely change your life!

Jesus answered, Verily, verily, I say unto thee, Except a man be born of water and of the Spirit, he cannot enter into the kingdom of God. That which is born of the flesh is flesh; and that which is born of the Spirit is spirit. Marvel not that I said unto thee, Ye must be born again. The wind bloweth where it listeth, and thou hearest the sound thereof, but canst not tell whence it cometh, and whither it goeth: so is every one that is born of the Spirit.

—John 3:5–8

1357. Everyone dies eventually, no matter how much noise we make, while kicking and screaming along the way. So we need to make the most of our years in life, and make our time and years count.

Whatsoever thy hand findeth to do, do it with thy might; for there is no work, nor device, nor knowledge, nor wisdom, in the grave, whither thou goest.

—Ecclesiastes 9:10

1358. Watching certain news networks is like *panning for gold* in a stream. You must keep the nuggets, but shake out the sand.

The simple believeth every word: but the prudent man looketh well to his going.

—Proverbs 14:15

1359. Don't you worry about not having enough. When no one else has anything, you will have something. There's *"Light in Goshen!"*

And the Lord said unto Moses, Stretch out thine hand toward heaven, that there may be darkness over the land of Egypt, even darkness which may be felt. And Moses stretched forth his hand toward heaven; and there was a thick darkness in all the land of Egypt three days: They saw not one another, neither rose any from his place for three days: but all the children of Israel had light in their dwellings.

—Exodus 10:21–23

A thousand shall fall at thy side, and ten thousand at thy right hand; but it shall not come nigh thee. Only with thine eyes shalt thou behold and see the reward of the wicked. Because thou hast made the Lord, which is my refuge, even the most High, thy habitation; There shall no evil befall thee, neither shall any plague come nigh thy dwelling.

—Psalm 91:7–10

1360. The effectual, fervent prayers of the righteous avails and prevails much in a nation, in the weather, in the economy,

in society, in the home, in a marriage. Never doubt the power of prayer, and never neglect it.

Confess your faults one to another, and pray one for another, that ye may be healed. The effectual fervent prayer of a righteous man availeth much. Elias was a man subject to like passions as we are, and he prayed earnestly that it might not rain: and it rained not on the earth by the space of three years and six months. And he prayed again, and the heaven gave rain, and the earth brought forth her fruit.

—James 5:16–18

And he spake a parable unto them *to this end*, that men ought always to pray, and not to faint.

—Luke 18:1

The sacrifice of the wicked is an abomination to the Lord: but the prayer of the upright is his delight.

—Proverbs 15:8

The Lord is far from the wicked: but he heareth the prayer of the righteous.

—Proverbs 15:29

I exhort therefore, that, first of all, supplications, prayers, intercessions, and giving of thanks, be made for all men; For kings, and for all that are in authority; that we may lead a quiet and peaceable life in all godliness and honesty.

—1 Timothy 2:1–2

1361. There's nothing like a gift to keep a home happy!

A gift is as a precious stone in the eyes of him that hath it: whithersoever it turneth, it prospereth.

—Proverbs 17:8

1362. Life is difficult, but two are better than one.

Two are better than one; because they have a good reward for their labour. For if they fall, the one will lift up his fellow: but woe to him that is alone when he falleth; for he hath not another to help him up. Again, if two lie together, then they have heat: but how can one be warm alone? And if one prevail against him, two shall withstand him; and a threefold cord is not quickly broken.

—Ecclesiastes 4:9–12

1363. Consideration is the key to living in polite society.

Let nothing be done through strife or vainglory; but in lowliness of mind let each esteem other better than themselves.

—Philippians 2:3

1364. At one time you may have been counting the gray hairs. Now you are counting the years. The better past-time is

to rather experience the joy and gratitude of counting our many blessings.

I have been young, and now am old; yet have I not seen the righteous forsaken, nor his seed begging bread.

—Psalm 37:25

1365. When faced with a decision, choice, or challenge, always take the road of faith.

But without faith it is impossible to please him: for he that cometh to God must believe that he is, and that he is a rewarder of them that diligently seek him.

—Hebrews 11:6

1366. Always pray during a transition. It takes time to allow the dust to settle. Keep plowing the ground in prayer, and planting seeds of love and faith. Trust God. He knows how to turn things out for our good. But, we can't give up. We must remain sober, watchful, and vigilant. God has it in His hands, but we must continue to stay involved.

And we know that all things work together for good to them that love God, to them who are the called according to his purpose.

—Romans 8:28

1367. We can't stop the impending years of aging. Therefore, we must determine to get better with age. Keep

feeding your faith, and keep on achieving courageous, noble deeds. Keep cultivating your mind with knowledge, information, and practicing wisdom. So that when you reach a certain age, you will be the perfect age *internally* to meet your life's new opportunities and challenges.

I have been young, and now am old; yet have I not seen the righteous forsaken, nor his seed begging bread. He is ever merciful, and lendeth; and his seed is blessed.

—Psalm 37:25–26

1368. Life is good, and it's getting better!

They go from strength to strength, every one of them in Zion appeareth before God.

—Psalm 84:7

1369. May The Church's vigilant mission continually be to engage in the exercise of fervent prayer. Thus, we will be preventing attacks of calamity, rather than, reacting to them once they have already occurred. This is our job. We've got the power!

And I will give unto thee the keys of the kingdom of heaven: and whatsoever thou shalt bind on earth shall be bound in heaven: and whatsoever thou shalt loose on earth shall be loosed in heaven.

—Matthew 16:19

1370. May we all pray for a safe and Happy Thanksgiving!

I exhort therefore, that, first of all, supplications, prayers, intercessions, and giving of thanks, be made for all men; For kings, and for all that are in authority; that we may lead a quiet and peaceable life in all godliness and honesty.

–1 Timothy 2:1–2

1371. Always pray regarding people, places, and events.

And he spake a parable unto them *to this end*, that men ought always to pray, and not to faint.

—Luke 18:1

1372. God is good all the time, whether we are good or not. However, when we are good, we get all the benefits of obeying His Word.

For I am the Lord, I change not; therefore ye sons of Jacob are not consumed.

—Malachi 3:6

Blessed be the Lord, who daily loadeth us with benefits, even the God of our salvation. Selah.

—Psalm 68:19

It is of the Lord's mercies that we are not consumed, because his compassions fail not. They are new every morning: great is thy faithfulness.

—Lamentations 3:22–23

1373. Listen with two sets of ears. See, with two sets of eyes. Discern with both your heart and your mind.

And the spirit of the Lord shall rest upon him, the spirit of wisdom and understanding, the spirit of counsel and might, the spirit of knowledge and of the fear of the Lord; And shall make him of quick understanding in the fear of the Lord: and he shall not judge after the sight of his eyes, neither reprove after the hearing of his ears: But with righteousness shall he judge the poor, and reprove with equity for the meek of the earth: and he shall smite the earth: with the rod of his mouth, and with the breath of his lips shall he slay the wicked. And righteousness shall be the girdle of his loins, and faithfulness the girdle of his reins.

—Isaiah 11:2–5

1374. Instruction delivers us from destruction.

My people are destroyed for lack of knowledge: because thou hast rejected knowledge, I will also reject thee, that thou shalt be no priest to me: seeing thou hast forgotten the law of thy God, I will also forget thy children.

—Hosea 4:6

1375. Many have gone before you that didn't have the knowledge or opportunities that you and I have. And there are many that succeeded in spite of their limitations. There are no excuses for us, but the excuses we accept.

Whatsoever thy hand findeth to do, do it with thy might; for there is no work, nor device, nor knowledge, nor wisdom, in the grave, whither thou goest.

—Ecclesiastes 9:10

1376. Your faith won't work like magic, but your faith will work, if you will work.

Even so faith, if it hath not works, is dead, being alone. Yea, a man may say, Thou hast faith, and I have works: shew me thy faith without thy works, and I will shew thee my faith by my works.

—James 2:17–18

1377. Your action is the only substance that reveals what you hope for. It is the only evidence that others have of what we do not see. Your action reveals what you believe to receive. Though we cannot see the object of your hope yet.

Even so faith, if it hath not works, is dead, being alone. Yea, a man may say, Thou hast faith, and I have works: shew me thy faith without thy works, and I will shew thee my faith by my works.

—James 2:17–18

1378. If you are born-again, your spirit belongs to God. You are hid in Christ Jesus. However, your soul is vulnerable to impressions. Either you will diligently choose what you focus on, or the world will.

Love not the world, neither the things that are in the world. If any man love the world, the love of the Father is not in him. For all that is in the world, the lust of the flesh, and the lust of the eyes, and the pride of life, is not of the Father, but is of the world. And the world passeth away, and the lust thereof: but he that doeth the will of God abideth for ever. Little children, it is the last time: and as ye have heard that antichrist shall come, even now are there many antichrists; whereby we know that it is the last time.

–1 John 2:15–18

1379. Your associations will determine your location. Birds of a feather flock together. And the flock usually ends up in the same place.

He that walketh with wise men shall be wise: but a companion of fools shall be destroyed.

—Proverbs 13:20

Simon Peter, a servant and an apostle of Jesus Christ, to them that have obtained like precious faith with us through the righteousness of God and our Saviour Jesus Christ.

—2 Peter 1:1

Be not deceived: evil communications corrupt good manners.

—1 Corinthians 15:33

1380. Some racists preach in Jesus' name, rather than love with Jesus' heart. If some, so called Christians, really loved with Jesus' heart by actually obeying the true spirit of the scripture, the world could really be a better place.

Having a form of godliness, but denying the power thereof: from such turn away.

—2 Timothy 3:5

1381. Unreleased potential fails to benefit you.

But without faith it is impossible to please him: for he that cometh to God must believe that he is, and that he is a rewarder of them that diligently seek him.

—Hebrews 11:6

1382. You may feel like a recent graduate of "Adversity University". You may have just received your Master's degree in problem-solving. Just think of it as preparation for life's greater challenges and opportunities, for which you wouldn't have been prepared if you didn't take the prior courses.

If thou faint in the day of adversity, thy strength is small.

—Proverbs 24:10

1383. Keep your head up and stay honest. Don't drop the ball now by allowing yourself to descend below the standard you have been raised with. You have too much to lose now, to not gain what your life deserves.

Be not deceived: evil communications corrupt good manners.

—1 Corinthians 15:33

1384. Be encouraged! Your destiny is too high and too great to be stopped by temporary situations. God is for you, God is with you, and God is in you, and there's no failure in God.

For our light affliction, which is but for a moment, worketh for us a far more exceeding and eternal weight of glory.

—2 Corinthians 4:17

1385. Regarding problems, when you've been through so much, you know that there is a *beginning* and an *end* to all problems. So, don't give up. This too will pass.

There hath no temptation taken you but such as is common to man: but God is faithful, who will not suffer you to be tempted above that ye are able; but will with the temptation also make a way to escape, that ye may be able to bear it.

—1 Corinthians 10:13

1386. Life is not static. Life is dynamic. You have to learn how to go with the flow, and flow with the go!

In the morning sow thy seed, and in the evening withhold not thine hand: for thou knowest not whether shall prosper, either this or that, or whether they both shall be alike good.

—Ecclesiastes 11:6

1387. Be sure to use your opportunity, to prepare for your opportunity, to be ready for your opportunity, when your opportunity comes.

There be four things which are little upon the earth, but they are exceeding wise: The ants are a people not strong, yet they prepare their meat in the summer.

—Proverbs 30:24–25

1388. What is the best vitamin for a Christian? B1. In fact, B1 is a multivitamin with multiple benefits. B1 is the perfect vitamin for all Christians.

Ye are the salt of the earth: but if the salt have lost his savour, wherewith shall it be salted? it is thenceforth good for nothing, but to be cast out, and to be trodden under foot of men. Ye are the light of the world. A city that is set on an hill cannot be hid. Neither do men light a candle, and put it under a bushel, but on a candlestick; and it giveth light unto all that are in the house. Let your light so shine before men, that they

may see your good works, and glorify your Father which is in heaven.

—Matthew 5:13–16

1389. One thing about faith is, if you will prepare for the future that you're believing for, God will hasten its arrival. Your faith will determine how quickly your future comes. If you want to be a singer, start singing. If you want to be a writer, start writing. If you want to live, start eating right and exercising. If you prepare for the future you desire, God will hasten its arrival.

Now faith is the substance of things hoped for, the evidence of things not seen. For by it the elders obtained a good report.

—Hebrews 11:1-2

1390. You have been called for such a time as this! You are a celebration!

For if thou altogether holdest thy peace at this time, then shall there enlargement and deliverance arise to the Jews from another place; but thou and thy father's house shall be destroyed: and who knoweth whether thou art come to the kingdom for such a time as this?

—Esther 4:14

1391. You're a champion! In spite of the continual challenges you may be facing, you are victorious. Just keep on

fighting. A reigning champion keeps on fighting. A retired champion is retired. Keep fighting!

For our light affliction, which is but for a moment, worketh for us a far more exceeding and eternal weight of glory.

–2 Corinthians 4:17

1392. You can walk through life calm, confident, cool, and collected when you know you have filled your heart with God's way of doing things, through meditating His Word.

And I will walk at liberty: for I seek thy precepts.

—Psalm 119:45

I will bless the Lord, who hath given me counsel: my reins also instruct me in the night seasons. I have set the Lord always before me: because he is at my right hand, I shall not be moved. Therefore my heart is glad, and my glory rejoiceth: my flesh also shall rest in hope.

—Psalm 16:7–9

1393. The more self-sufficient, self-aware, and self-reliant you are, the better. Once you realize what you have, the less dependent you are on others, and the better service you can be to others, because you know who you are.

But let every man prove his own work, and then shall he have rejoicing in himself alone, and not in another.

—Galatians 6:4

1394. Regarding being exceptional, if you can believe it, you can achieve it. If you can see it, you can be it, because you are it. You are only becoming the highest form of what you were preordained to be.

I will praise thee; for I am fearfully and wonderfully made: marvellous are thy works; and that my soul knoweth right well. My substance was not hid from thee, when I was made in secret, and curiously wrought in the lowest parts of the earth. Thine eyes did see my substance, yet being unperfect; and in thy book all my members were written, which in continuance were fashioned, when as yet there was none of them. How precious also are thy thoughts unto me, O God! how great is the sum of them! If I should count them, they are more in number than the sand: when I awake, I am still with thee.

—Psalm 139:14–18

1395. Regarding success, God always does His Part. It's us that often fail to do our part, but when we do, success is guaranteed!

And whatsoever ye do, do it heartily, as to the Lord, and not unto men; knowing that of the Lord ye shall receive the reward of the inheritance: for ye serve the Lord Christ.

—Colossians 3:23–24

1396. If your Bible is tore up from you reading it: you're not!

O how love I thy law! it is my meditation all the day. Thou through thy commandments hast made me wiser than mine enemies: for they are ever with me. I have more understanding than all my teachers: for thy testimonies are my meditation. I understand more than the ancients, because I keep thy precepts.

—Psalm 119:97–100

1397. Yeah, I hear what you're saying, but I see what you're doing, so I ain't hearing what you're saying.

Therefore whosoever heareth these sayings of mine, and doeth them, I will liken him unto a wise man, which built his house upon a rock: And the rain descended, and the floods came, and the winds blew, and beat upon that house; and it fell not: for it was founded upon a rock. And every one that heareth these sayings of mine, and doeth them not, shall be likened unto a foolish man, which built his house upon the sand: And the rain descended, and the floods came, and the winds blew, and beat upon that house; and it fell: and great was the fall of it.

—Matthew 7:24–27

1398. Often we spend time lamenting potential problems, yet if we spend that time interceding we could prevent many potential problems.

I exhort therefore, that, first of all, supplications, prayers, intercessions, and giving of thanks, be made for all men; For kings, and for all that are in authority; that we may lead a quiet and peaceable life in all godliness and honesty.

–1 Timothy 2:1–2

1399. God is the God of His perfect will. We assist the coming to pass of His perfect will in the earth through our prayers, obedience, and actions of faith.

The heaven, even the heavens, are the Lord's: but the earth hath he given to the children of men.

—Psalm 115:16

And I will give unto thee the keys of the kingdom of heaven: and whatsoever thou shalt bind on earth shall be bound in heaven: and whatsoever thou shalt loose on earth shall be loosed in heaven.

—Matthew 16:19

Out of the mouth of babes and sucklings hast thou ordained strength because of thine enemies, that thou mightest still the enemy and the avenger.

—Psalm 8:2

1400. The only people who fight against prosperity are those who no longer believe they will have any. They have settled for a lesser reality than what God originally planned

for them and have forfeited the "good fight of faith", which we are bound to win, if we fight lawfully and persevere.

Fight the good fight of faith, lay hold on eternal life, whereunto thou art also called, and hast professed a good profession before many witnesses.

—1 Timothy 6:12

1401. A good worker knows how to determine what's top priority without having to be told.

To every thing there is a season, and a time to every purpose under the heaven.

—Ecclesiastes 3:1

1402. The first key to success is to calm your mind, will, emotions, and body, and to decide to focus on a particular outcome. Focus on reading and studying a particular subject. Take continual, gradual action towards it, and never give up. You will grow as you go, and you will already be a success when you become a success.

Wisdom is the principal thing; therefore get wisdom: and with all thy getting get understanding.

—Proverbs 4:7

1403. Some people can cerebrally analyze and discuss things without end, seemingly having all the answers; yet they

lack the soul of the issue, and never can touch or grasp the true essence.

And Elihu the son of Barachel the Buzite answered and said, I am young, and ye are very old; wherefore I was afraid, and durst not shew you mine opinion. I said, Days should speak, and multitude of years should teach wisdom. But there is a spirit in man: and the inspiration of the Almighty giveth them understanding. Great men are not always wise: neither do the aged understand judgment.

—Job 32:6–9

1404. Enjoy the process, because the destiny is sure.

Then the Word of the Lord came unto me, saying, Before I formed thee in the belly I knew thee; and before thou camest forth out of the womb I sanctified thee, and I ordained thee a prophet unto the nations.

—Jeremiah 1:4–5

1405. Be confident in God's Word to you. God doesn't forget what He said, and He doesn't play. If He said it, He will bring it to pass. If He promised it, He will fulfill it. Just be courageous, committed, and strong. And, remain engaged in your own destiny.

God is not a man, that he should lie; neither the son of man, that he should repent: hath he said, and shall he not do it? or hath he spoken, and shall he not make it good?

—Numbers 23:19

1406. Singing praise and worship to God clears the *airspace*. It causes the satanic enemies of God's kingdom to scatter!

Let God arise, let his enemies be scattered: let them also that hate him flee before him.

—Psalm 68:1

1407. Savor celebrations. There are so many petty things we could complain about, and yes, there are some really major problems in life. Therefore, we should take every opportunity to savor celebrations. Have a Merry Christmas!

For unto you is born this day in the city of David a Saviour, which is Christ the Lord. And this *shall be a* sign unto you; Ye shall find the babe wrapped in swaddling clothes, lying in a manger. And suddenly there was with the angel a multitude of the heavenly host praising God, and saying, Glory to God in the highest, and on earth peace, good will toward men.

—Luke 2:11–14

1408. When life is not perfect, and it's not as good as you want it to be, you must *"squeeze all of the juice"* out of every bit of good that you can, and savor every moment! Merry Christmas!

Then he said unto them, Go your way, eat the fat, and drink the sweet, and send portions unto them for whom nothing is

prepared: for this day is holy unto our Lord: neither be ye sorry; for the joy of the Lord is your strength.

—Nehemiah 8:10

1409. Once you seek excellence for the sake of excellence and no longer perform for the sake of impressing others or out of fear, you have reached a new place of freedom. You are entering into your God-likeness.

Then said Jesus to those Jews which believed on him, If ye continue in my word, then are ye my disciples indeed; and ye shall know the truth, and the truth shall make you free.

—John 8:31–32

1410. Ask God to help you live out of love and liberty, and not fear. You will feel so much better!

Now the Lord is that Spirit: and where the Spirit of the Lord is, there is liberty.

−2 Corinthians 3:17

There is no fear in love; but perfect love casteth out fear: because fear hath torment. He that feareth is not made perfect in love.

−1 John 4:18

1411. Every Christian should live between two intense realities: "Occupy until I come", and "Even so come Lord

Jesus". It's the only way to remain relevant while we're here, and the only way to be ready for Jesus' hastening return.

He said therefore, A certain nobleman went into a far country to receive for himself a kingdom, and to return. And he called his ten servants, and delivered them ten pounds, and said unto them, Occupy till I come.

—Luke 19:12–13

Take ye heed, watch and pray: for ye know not when the time is. For the Son of Man is as a man taking a far journey, who left his house, and gave authority to his servants, and to every man his work, and commanded the porter to watch. Watch ye therefore: for ye know not when the master of the house cometh, at even, or at midnight, or at the cockcrowing, or in the morning: Lest coming suddenly he find you sleeping. And what I say unto you I say unto all, Watch.

—Mark 13:33–37

He which testifieth these things saith, Surely I come quickly. Amen. Even so, come, Lord Jesus.

—Revelation 22:20

1412. Every Christian should spend their time speaking only in the affirmative of what God's Word, The Bible, says. Otherwise, we should pray in The Holy Ghost, rather than complain. This is the only way to live in God's perfect will, without giving place to the devil.

Neither give place to the devil.

—Ephesians 4:27

The centurion answered and said, Lord, I am not worthy that thou shouldest come under my roof: but speak the Word only, and my servant shall be healed.

—Matthew 8:8

For he that speaketh in an unknown tongue speaketh not unto men, but unto God: for no man understandeth him; howbeit in the spirit he speaketh mysteries.

–1 Corinthians 14:2

1413. If you realize that you need Jesus now more than ever, call on Him now. He will surely answer you every time.

For whosoever shall call upon the name of the Lord shall be saved.

—Romans 10:13

1414. Keep on producing. Even when it takes time to get the reward. Nothing goes to waste when you do it with excellence!

In the morning sow thy seed, and in the evening withhold not thine hand: for thou knowest not whether shall prosper, either this or that, or whether they both shall be alike good.

—Ecclesiastes 11:6

1415. There's nothing that can be said against *done*. Especially if it's a comment that's coming from someone who is not doing anything!

Even so faith, if it hath not works, is dead, being alone. Yea, a man may say, Thou hast faith, and I have works: shew me thy faith without thy works, and I will shew thee my faith by my works.

—James 2:17–18

1416. Don't be concerned with competing with the minute minority of people in your field that are competing for the same jobs or business. Rather, focus on serving the remaining majority of billions of customers that can't do or make what you have to offer, and serve them with your special gift, talent, or product.

Give, and it shall be given unto you; good measure, pressed down, and shaken together, and running over, shall men give into your bosom. For with the same measure that ye mete withal it shall be measured to you again.

—Luke 6:38

1417. Regarding courage, risk your life to live. Do not risk your life to die.

I beseech you therefore, brethren, by the mercies of God, that ye present your bodies a living sacrifice, holy, acceptable unto God, which is your reasonable service. And be not conformed to this world: but be ye transformed by the renewing of your mind, that ye may prove what is that good, and acceptable, and perfect, will of God.

—Romans 12:1–2

1418. It's Christmas time. Love is in the air. Love is more than a feeling. Love is doing the right things, simply because you care. Love is sacrificing feelings, to express your true intentions. Love goes deeper than what mere words could mention. Do the most you can to show others how much you care. It's Christmas time. Love is in the air. Merry Christmas!

For God so loved the world, that he gave his only begotten Son, that whosoever believeth in him should not perish, but have everlasting life. For God sent not his Son into the world to condemn the world; but that the world through him might be saved.

—John 3:16–17

Then he said unto them, Go your way, eat the fat, and drink the sweet, and send portions unto them for whom nothing is prepared: for this day is holy unto our Lord: neither be ye sorry; for the joy of the Lord is your strength.

—Nehemiah 8:10

1419. It's never good to say definitely about possibly.

He that answereth a matter before he heareth it, it is folly and shame unto him.

—Proverbs 18:13

1420. We should eat like kings and queens this Christmas season and into the New Year. They eat the healthiest food to stay healthy and alive. Eat healthy food like you have an entire kingdom depending on your healthy body and mind. Your health enables your ability to make good decisions and serve your family, friends, community, nation, and world. Merry Christmas!

And God said, Behold, I have given you every herb bearing seed, which is upon the face of all the earth, and every tree, in the which is the fruit of a tree yielding seed; to you it shall be for meat.

—Genesis 1:29

1421. The closer you get to the timing of your divine destiny, the greater the release of the anointing for your divine destiny.

But we all, with open face beholding as in a glass the glory of the Lord, are changed into the same image from glory to glory, even as by the Spirit of the Lord.

—2 Corinthians 3:18

They go from strength to strength, every one of them in Zion appeareth before God.

—Psalm 84:7

1422. Failures become critics.

He that is despised, and hath a servant, is better than he that honoureth himself, and lacketh bread.

—Proverbs 12:9

1423. During the debate is when things can be contested. After a decision has been made is when a thing should be supported.

Fulfil ye my joy, that ye be likeminded, having the same love, being of one accord, of one mind.

—Philippians 2:2

1424. In the *school of life*, sometimes testing is teaching. The answers to the lesson can be found in the details of the questions.

I will instruct thee and teach thee in the way which thou shalt go: I will guide thee with mine eye.

—Psalm 32:8

1425. You don't have to be big, to be big.

For who hath despised the day of small things? for they shall rejoice, and shall see the plummet in the hand of Zerubbabel with those seven; they are the eyes of the Lord, which run to and fro through the whole earth.

—Zechariah 4:10

And Jonathan said to the young man that bare his armour, Come, and let us go over unto the garrison of these uncircumcised: it may be that the Lord will work for us: for there is no restraint to the Lord to save by many or by few. And his armourbearer said unto him, Do all that is in thine heart: turn thee; behold, I am with thee according to thy heart.

—1 Samuel 14:6–7

1426. Life isn't about perfection. Life is about progression. Don't be discouraged if everything in your life is not perfect. Just keep going forward. Keep moving forward! You will accomplish more than you ever thought possible! Life is not about perfection. Life is about progression.

Brethren, I count not myself to have apprehended: but this one thing I do, forgetting those things which are behind, and reaching forth unto those things which are before, I press toward the mark for the prize of the high calling of God in Christ Jesus.

—Philippians 3:13–14

1427. Trouble makes you pray more, but if you'll pray more, you'll have less trouble.

And he spake a parable unto them *to this end*, that men ought always to pray, and not to faint.

—Luke 18:1

Watch and pray, that ye enter not into temptation: the spirit indeed is willing, but the flesh is weak.

—Matthew 26:41

1428. Regarding people, always remember, if the dog has teeth, the dog will bite!

When thou sittest to eat with a ruler, consider diligently what is before thee: And put a knife to thy throat, if thou be a man given to appetite. Be not desirous of his dainties: for they are deceitful meat. Labour not to be rich: cease from thine own wisdom. Wilt thou set thine eyes upon that which is not? for riches certainly make themselves wings; they fly away as an eagle toward heaven. Eat thou not the bread of him that hath an evil eye, neither desire thou his dainty meats: For as he thinketh in his heart, so is he: Eat and drink, saith he to thee; but his heart is not with thee. The morsel which thou hast eaten shalt thou vomit up, and lose thy sweet words.

—Proverbs 23:1–8

The simple believeth every word: but the prudent man looketh well to his going.

—Proverbs 14:15

1429. Good credit is walking in the blessing, and working to have enough to pay for what you want. Rather than, going into debt and slavery to pay back someone for endless years.

The rich ruleth over the poor, and the borrower is servant to the lender.

—Proverbs 22:7

Owe no man any thing, but to love one another: for he that loveth another hath fulfilled the law.

—Romans 13:8

The Lord shall open unto thee his good treasure, the heaven to give the rain unto thy land in his season, and to bless all the work of thine hand: and thou shalt lend unto many nations, and thou shalt not borrow.

—Deuteronomy 28:12

A good man sheweth favour, and lendeth: he will guide his affairs with discretion.

—Psalm 112:5

1430. You and I owe it to all the *"great cloud of witnesses"* both in Heaven and on Earth, who have gone before us, and that surround us, to live honorably, and to strive to live out the fulfillment of all of God's promises, which are *"yes and amen"* to all them that believe.

Wherefore seeing we also are compassed about with so great a cloud of witnesses, let us lay aside every weight, and the sin which doth so easily beset us, and let us run with patience the race that is set before us, Looking unto Jesus the author and finisher of our faith; who for the joy that was set before him endured the cross, despising the shame, and is set down at the right hand of the throne of God. For consider him that endured such contradiction of sinners against himself, lest ye be wearied and faint in your minds. Ye have not yet resisted unto blood, striving against sin.

—Hebrews 12:1–4

1431. If you've started your business or produced your valuable product, then rejoice! Your million's of dollars are in the pipeline! It will be just a matter of time, faith, and effort. Fight until the finish, and systematically use the proven natural techniques to bring in your harvest. Also, continue to use spiritual principles of prayer, fasting, worship, and the Word. You will release your profit out of the pipeline!

Thus saith the Lord, thy Redeemer, the Holy One of Israel; I am the Lord thy God which teacheth thee to profit, which leadeth thee by the way that thou shouldest go.

—Isaiah 48:17

And that ye study to be quiet, and to do your own business, and to work with your own hands, as we commanded you; that ye may walk honestly toward them that are without, and that ye may have lack of nothing.

—1 Thessalonians 4:11–12

1432. If you can see big, you can be big!

For as he thinketh in his heart, so is he...

—Proverbs 23:7a

1433. Champions overcome. Losers lose. If it seems like you've been going against a challenge, and you've been overcoming and overcoming, and going against it and going against it, and you're still standing, then it means you're getting stronger and tougher, and not weaker. Champions overcome. Losers lose.

Be ye strong therefore, and let not your hands be weak: for your work shall be rewarded.

—2 Chronicles 15:7

1434. The greatest teachers are profitable practitioners of their lessons learned. They are proof positive of their wisdom gained.

The crown of the wise is their riches: but the foolishness of fools is folly.

—Proverbs 14:24

1435. The person who diligently seeks to do good procures favor like compound interest.

He that diligently seeketh good procureth favour: but he that seeketh mischief, it shall come unto him.

—Proverbs 11:27

1436. Don't fight the inevitable. Shape the malleable. In other words, don't fight what you can't change. Change what you can change.

Whatsoever thy hand findeth to do, do it with thy might; for there is no work, nor device, nor knowledge, nor wisdom, in the grave, whither thou goest. I returned, and saw under the sun, that the race is not to the swift, nor the battle to the strong, neither yet bread to the wise, nor yet riches to men of understanding, nor yet favour to men of skill; but time and chance happeneth to them all.

—Ecclesiastes 9:10–11

1437. The reasons to praise the Lord keep adding up, just like the years! Keep on praising the Lord, and have a Happy New Year!

Blessed be the Lord, who daily loadeth us with benefits, even the God of our salvation. Selah.

—Psalm 68:19

1438. In regards to dreams and visions, take time to get a clear vision for your life. Find out exactly what you want. For

when you know exactly what you want, the fulfillment comes much faster!

And they said, Go to, let us build us a city and a tower, whose top may reach unto heaven; and let us make us a name, lest we be scattered abroad upon the face of the whole earth. And the Lord came down to see the city and the tower, which the children of men builded. And the Lord said, Behold, the people is one, and they have all one language; and this they begin to do: and now nothing will be restrained from them, which they have imagined to do.

—Genesis 11:4–6

1439. You can't stay small, when you see big!

For as he thinketh in his heart, so is he...

—Proverbs 23:7a

1440. There's power in victorious preaching! If you can see higher, you can be higher!

For I am not ashamed of the gospel of Christ: for it is the power of God unto salvation to every one that believeth; to the Jew first, and also to the Greek. For therein is the righteousness of God revealed from faith to faith: as it is written, The just shall live by faith.

—Romans 1:16–17

But we all, with open face beholding as in a glass the glory of the Lord, are changed into the same image from glory to glory, even as by the Spirit of the Lord.

—2 Corinthians 3:18

They go from strength to strength, every one of them in Zion appeareth before God.

—Psalm 84:7

1441. Husbands and wives wear their "*seventy times seven*" card on their left ring finger. That's the true "*get out of jail free card*". Or, off the sofa!

Then came Peter to him, and said, Lord, how oft shall my brother sin against me, and I forgive him? till seven times? Jesus saith unto him, I say not unto thee, Until seven times: but, Until seventy times seven.

—Matthew 18:21–22

1442. The way to make money is to be smarter than your customer. The way to keep more of your money is to be smarter than the seller. Thus, the equalizer between the two is knowledge. Love and respect will determine how the deal turns out when the balance of knowledge is equal.

It is naught, it is naught, saith the buyer: but when he is gone his way, then he boasteth.

—Proverbs 20:14

Let nothing be done through strife or vainglory; but in lowliness of mind let each esteem other better than themselves.

—Philippians 2:3

1443. The money is in the pipeline! And it's coming through!

In all labour there is profit: but the talk of the lips tendeth only to penury.

—Proverbs 14:23

1444. Clouds always attempt to block the shining stars. Yet, stars continue to rise and shine higher in the open sky.

And Saul was afraid of David, because the Lord was with him, and was departed from Saul. Therefore Saul removed him from him, and made him his captain over a thousand; and he went out and came in before the people. And David behaved himself wisely in all his ways; and the Lord was with him. Wherefore when Saul saw that he behaved himself very wisely, he was afraid of him. But all Israel and Judah loved David, because he went out and came in before them.

—1 Samuel 18:12–16

1445. The best thing that a young person can do is to learn to love and serve the Lord at an early age. Make Him the foundation of your life. Let your love for Him grow stronger

and purer each day. He will uphold you and keep you during the storms of life, and you will be the head and not the tail and have a good reputation and true success in life.

Remember now thy Creator in the days of thy youth, while the evil days come not, nor the years draw nigh, when thou shalt say, I have no pleasure in them.

—Ecclesiastes 12:1

Wherewithal shall a young man cleanse his way? by taking heed thereto according to thy word.

—Psalm 119:9

And that from a child thou hast known the holy scriptures, which are able to make thee wise unto salvation through faith which is in Christ Jesus.

−2 Timothy 3:15

1446. Concerning business, home, and life we should have the same aspirations as Oprah Winfrey: OWN!

And that ye study to be quiet, and to do your own business, and to work with your own hands, as we commanded you; that ye may walk honestly toward them that are without, and that ye may have lack of nothing.

−1 Thessalonians 4:11–12

1447. Just like Oprah Winfrey had the aspiration and ambition to keep striving past her initial talent and profession as a talk show host, in order to own her own network, magazine, production studio, etc.; we too should keep striving for ownership of all we have the capacity of acquiring in life. We shouldn't settle for less than we deserve and have a right to.

And that ye study to be quiet, and to do your own business, and to work with your own hands, as we commanded you; that ye may walk honestly toward them that are without, and that ye may have lack of nothing.

–1 Thessalonians 4:11–12

1448. The person who works to gather, in the *summer* of life, will have a harvest in the *winter* of life, when the snow starts to gather on your head, as the hairs turn white. Make the most of each day to ensure a sustaining harvest when the seasons of life change.

He becometh poor that dealeth with a slack hand: but the hand of the diligent maketh rich. He that gathereth in summer is a wise son: but he that sleepeth in harvest is a son that causeth shame.

—Proverbs 10:4–5

1449. We should thank God for every good thing in our lives, and everything that God has given us is good. It's a way

of maintaining joy, and even if you're not feeling joy, it's a way of stirring up some joy!

Every good gift and every perfect gift is from above, and cometh down from the Father of lights, with whom is no variableness, neither shadow of turning.

—James 1:17

It is a good thing to give thanks unto the Lord, and to sing praises unto thy name, O Most High: To shew forth thy lovingkindness in the morning, and thy faithfulness every night.

—Psalm 92:1–2

1450. Always assume the best until proven otherwise, and even if it is proven otherwise, God can always work all things together for your good.

And we know that all things work together for good to them that love God, to them who are the called according to his purpose.

—Romans 8:28

1451. Only when you seriously consider the prospect of your life coming to an end, will you seriously consider making the most of the rest of your life. Your days are numbered. Therefore, decide what's most important, and commit to making the rest of your life, the best of your life.

Whatsoever thy hand findeth to do, do it with thy might; for there is no work, nor device, nor knowledge, nor wisdom, in the grave, whither thou goest.

—Ecclesiastes 9:10

1452. History can be kind to heroes, but cruel to *zeros*. We each must decide what side of history we want to be on. "Who's on The Lord's side?" Stand up. Stand out. Make a difference.

Then Moses stood in the gate of the camp, and said, Who is on the Lord's side? let him come unto me. And all the sons of Levi gathered themselves together unto him.

—Exodus 32:26

1453. In business and in life, discussions that were not written down didn't happen. Expressions of love in romantic relationships that don't lead to a written marriage license don't count. Contracts discussed, yet not documented, are not usually binding. Visions not clearly written are not fully executed. In business and in life, discussions that are not written down didn't happen.

And the Lord answered me, and said, Write the vision, and make it plain upon tables, that he may run that readeth it. For the vision is yet for an appointed time, but at the end it shall speak, and not lie: though it tarry, wait for it; because it will surely come, it will not tarry. Behold, his soul which is lifted up is not upright in him: but the just shall live by his faith.

—Habakkuk 2:2–4

1454. Take time to dream, set goals, and plan beyond your natural ability to reach or control. Then let go of the reins of the chariot, and let God take you on the ride of a lifetime!

A man's heart deviseth his way: but the Lord directeth his steps.

—Proverbs 16:9

1455. This is the day that the Lord has made. Let us rejoice and be glad in it! This is another opportunity to give Him thanks for all the abundant blessings He has bestowed upon us like food to eat, a bed to sleep in, hot water to take a bath, water to drink, a home to live in, and so much more! Take time to praise Him at the beginning of each day. You will start in victory! God bless you!

In every thing give thanks: for this is the will of God in Christ Jesus concerning you.

−1 Thessalonians 5:18

1456. Faith is taking action on what you believe to achieve, which is what you hope for. It's the only way to please God, for it is the only way to succeed. And, God wishes above all things that we prosper or succeed, be in health, even as our souls prosper.

Distinguished Wisdom Presents . . . "Living Proverbs"–Vol.3

But without faith it is impossible to please him: for he that cometh to God must believe that he is, and that he is a rewarder of them that diligently seek him.

—Hebrews 11:6

Beloved, I wish above all things that thou mayest prosper and be in health, even as thy soul prospereth.

–3 John 2

1457. Regarding goal achievement, focus on finishing, because you never know when you're finished.

Whatsoever thy hand findeth to do, do it with thy might; for there is no work, nor device, nor knowledge, nor wisdom, in the grave, whither thou goest. I returned, and saw under the sun, that the race is not to the swift, nor the battle to the strong, neither yet bread to the wise, nor yet riches to men of understanding, nor yet favour to men of skill; but time and chance happeneth to them all. For man also knoweth not his time: as the fishes that are taken in an evil net, and as the birds that are caught in the snare; so are the sons of men snared in an evil time, when it falleth suddenly upon them. This wisdom have I seen also under the sun, and it seemed great unto me.

—Ecclesiastes 9:10–13

1458. When you don't see a sign, trust God's Word. To believe and rely on His Word, in absence of a sign or feeling, is a sign to Him of your maturity. But, believe and know, He will never leave you nor forsake you. He will comfort you,

and let you know He's by your side. Press into what you already know, until of the sign comes.

I do set my bow in the cloud, and it shall be for a token of a covenant between me and the earth. And it shall come to pass, when I bring a cloud over the earth, that the bow shall be seen in the cloud: And I will remember my covenant, which is between me and you and every living creature of all flesh; and the waters shall no more become a flood to destroy all flesh. And the bow shall be in the cloud; and I will look upon it, that I may remember the everlasting covenant between God and every living creature of all flesh that is upon the earth. And God said unto Noah, This is the token of the covenant, which I have established between me and all flesh that is upon the earth.

—Genesis 9:13–17

1459. Learning is just as important as earning. Take time to learn, so that you will be more prepared to earn.

He that getteth wisdom loveth his own soul: he that keepeth understanding shall find good.

—Proverbs 19:8

1460. Remember that whether you accomplish all you want today or not, every step in the right direction is a step in the right direction. Keep progressing, and have a productive day!

The steps of a good man are ordered by the Lord: and he delighteth in his way.

—Psalm 37:23

1461. This is a time when God will show His good hand of favor upon His children. Those who have stood for His name and principles, and exercised His laws of success, will taste the fruit of your labor. The environment may not appear perfect, but God is. He knows how to show the difference between the righteous and the unrighteous. Be encouraged.

Thus saith the Lord God; When I shall have gathered the house of Israel from the people among whom they are scattered, and shall be sanctified in them in the sight of the heathen, then shall they dwell in their land that I have given to my servant Jacob. And they shall dwell safely therein, and shall build houses, and plant vineyards; yea, they shall dwell with confidence, when I have executed judgments upon all those that despise them round about them; and they shall know that I am the Lord their God.

—Ezekiel 28:25–26

1462. In goal achievement, sometimes it seems that you expend so much fuel to get to the starting line during preparation time, that you may feel you don't have the energy to make the real journey. But, don't be deceived. The boosters that took you this far have given you enough momentum and direction to make the rest of the journey a guaranteed success!

He must increase, but I must decrease.

—John 3:30

1463. Reading, study, taking courses, etc.; helps to prepare you and I for greater earning power on our jobs and in our businesses. We should take time for continuous improvement in knowledge, skills, and information in order to be more profitable in life.

He that tilleth his land shall be satisfied with bread: but he that followeth vain persons is void of understanding.

—Proverbs 12:11

1464. Never give up! Keep pushing until you're pushing up daisies!

Fight the good fight of faith, lay hold on eternal life, whereunto thou art also called, and hast professed a good profession before many witnesses.

–1 Timothy 6:12

1465. Once you produce a crop, you must work hard to get the harvest in before winter.

He becometh poor that dealeth with a slack hand: but the hand of the diligent maketh rich. He that gathereth in summer is a wise son: but he that sleepeth in harvest is a son that causeth shame.

—Proverbs 10:4–5

1466. One of the ways to be successful is to read autobiographies of successful people. Then say, "If they could do it, I will too!" Then get busy studying how, and then, do what they did. Success is available to all!

And that ye study to be quiet, and to do your own business, and to work with your own hands, as we commanded you; that ye may walk honestly toward them that are without, and that ye may have lack of nothing.

—1 Thessalonians 4:11–12

1467. Make plans and get moving! Because the year moves really fast!

So teach us to number our days, that we may apply our hearts unto wisdom.

—Psalm 90:12

1468. Miracles happen sometimes. Principles happen all the time. Believe for miracles, but invest in principles.

And that ye study to be quiet, and to do your own business, and to work with your own hands, as we commanded you; that ye may walk honestly toward them that are without, and that ye may have lack of nothing.

—1 Thessalonians 4:11–12

Pastor Terrance Levise Turner, MBA

1469. Discomfort with where you are, causes you to move to where you should be!

If ye be willing and obedient, ye shall eat the good of the land.

—Isaiah 1:19

1470. Always be consistent in treating the people you know and see, well, because you could be someone's life-vest.

And be ye kind one to another, tenderhearted, forgiving one another, even as God for Christ's sake hath forgiven you.

—Ephesians 4:32

Love endures long *and* is patient and kind; love never is envious *nor* boils over with jealousy, is not boastful *or* vainglorious, does not display itself haughtily. It is not conceited (arrogant and inflated with pride); it is not rude (unmannerly) *and* does not act unbecomingly. Love (God's love in us) does not insist on its own rights *or* its own way, *for* it is not self-seeking; it is not touchy *or* fretful *or* resentful; it takes no account of the evil done to it [it pays no attention to a suffered wrong]. It does not rejoice at injustice *and* unrighteousness, but rejoices when right *and* truth prevail. Love bears up under anything *and* everything that comes, is ever ready to believe the best of every person, its hopes are fadeless under all circumstances, and it endures everything [without weakening]. Love never fails [never fades out or becomes obsolete or comes to an end]. As for prophecy (the gift of interpreting the divine will

and purpose), it will be fulfilled *and* pass away; as for tongues, they will be destroyed *and* cease; as for knowledge, it will pass away [it will lose its value and be superseded by truth].

—1 Corinthians 13:4–8

—Amplified Bible, Classic Edition (AMPC)

1471. When you're crazy enough to believe your dream, you need to get with someone who's crazy enough to believe their dream! You will be comfort to one another in your mutual quest!

Iron sharpeneth iron; so a man sharpeneth the countenance of his friend.

—Proverbs 27:17

1472. As a people, our hope and trust must always be upon God. We must submit ourselves to His principles and laws, and hope for His favor in all things regarding our nation. Pray for those in leadership. Obey God. Be of service. Love yourself and others. In Jesus name, amen.

I exhort therefore, that, first of all, supplications, prayers, intercessions, and giving of thanks, be made for all men; For kings, and for all that are in authority; that we may lead a quiet and peaceable life in all godliness and honesty.

—1 Timothy 2:1–2

1473. If it's raining cats and dogs, it must be purring Poodles!

And it came to pass at the seventh time, that he said, Behold, there ariseth a little cloud out of the sea, like a man's hand. And he said, Go up, say unto Ahab, Prepare thy chariot, and get thee down that the rain stop thee not. And it came to pass in the mean while, that the heaven was black with clouds and wind, and there was a great rain. And Ahab rode, and went to Jezreel.

–1 Kings 18:44–45

1474. The difference between a millionaire and a billionaire is a millionaire wants to cut expenses to save as much money as possible, because he or she remembers his or her struggle. A billionaire just wants the *best*, no matter what the expense, because he or she simply wants to *win*!

For as he thinketh in his heart, so is he...

—Proverbs 23:7a

And God gave Solomon wisdom and understanding exceeding much, and largeness of heart, even as the sand that is on the sea shore.

–1 Kings 4:29

And the king made silver and gold at Jerusalem as plenteous as stones, and cedar trees made he as the sycomore trees that are in the vale for abundance.

–2 Chronicles 1:15

1475. Regarding God's plans for you, it's not your responsibility to know the full plan. It is your responsibility to take the *next step*. That's called faith!

The steps of a good man are ordered by the Lord: and he delighteth in his way.

—Psalm 37:23

For we walk by faith, not by sight.

–2 Corinthians 5:7

1476. The key to forward progress is to *"bump brains"* with forward-thinking people!

He that walketh with wise men shall be wise: but a companion of fools shall be destroyed.

—Proverbs 13:20

1477. It's God's will that you succeed. So, if you're *willing* to succeed, you *will* succeed.

If ye be willing and obedient, ye shall eat the good of the land.

—Isaiah 1:19

1478. You can't defeat someone who's playing a different game.

And in nothing terrified by your adversaries: which is to them an evident token of perdition, but to you of salvation, and that of God.

—Philippians 1:28

1479. When God tells you to do something, go ahead, and step out in faith, even if you don't understand all the details. Just go! Then, study, listen, and learn as you go. He's revealing a miracle to you, by faith. First, you receive the promise; then, the obedience for the journey; and then, the total fulfillment for the reward. It's worth the journey!

Now the Lord had said unto Abram, Get thee out of thy country, and from thy kindred, and from thy father's house, unto a land that I will shew thee: And I will make of thee a great nation, and I will bless thee, and make thy name great; and thou shalt be a blessing: And I will bless them that bless thee, and curse him that curseth thee: and in thee shall all families of the earth be blessed. So Abram departed, as the Lord had spoken unto him; and Lot went with him: and Abram was seventy and five years old when he departed out of Haran. And Abram took Sarai his wife, and Lot his brother's son, and all their substance that they had gathered, and the souls that they had gotten in Haran; and they went forth to go into the land of Canaan; and into the land of Canaan they came.

—Genesis 12:1–5

1480. You should run your business like a frugal man eating a *hog*. Maximize every resource down to the bone, and leave nothing on the table!

After these things Jesus went over the sea of Galilee, which is the sea of Tiberias. And a great multitude followed him, because they saw his miracles which he did on them that were diseased. And Jesus went up into a mountain, and there he sat with his disciples. And the passover, a feast of the Jews, was nigh. When Jesus then lifted up his eyes, and saw a great company come unto him, he saith unto Philip, Whence shall we buy bread, that these may eat? And this he said to prove him: for he himself knew what he would do. Philip answered him, Two hundred pennyworth of bread is not sufficient for them, that every one of them may take a little. One of his disciples, Andrew, Simon Peter's brother, saith unto him, There is a lad here, which hath five barley loaves, and two small fishes: but what are they among so many? And Jesus said, Make the men sit down. Now there was much grass in the place. So the men sat down, in number about five thousand. And Jesus took the loaves; and when he had given thanks, he distributed to the disciples, and the disciples to them that were set down; and likewise of the fishes as much as they would. When they were filled, he said unto his disciples, Gather up the fragments that remain, that nothing be lost. Therefore they gathered them together, and filled twelve baskets with the fragments of the five barley loaves, which remained over and above unto them that had eaten.

—John 6:1–13

1481. A sign of maturity is to be able to successfully make it through seemingly *"end-of-the-world"* events without pulling your hair out, because you know the world will still be here in the morning!

My brethren, count it all joy when ye fall into divers temptations; Knowing this, that the trying of your faith worketh patience. But let patience have her perfect work, that ye may be perfect and entire, wanting nothing.

—James 1:2–4

1482. You are they, and you ought to do something.

Ye are the salt of the earth: but if the salt have lost his savour, wherewith shall it be salted? it is thenceforth good for nothing, but to be cast out, and to be trodden under foot of men. Ye are the light of the world. A city that is set on an hill cannot be hid. Neither do men light a candle, and put it under a bushel, but on a candlestick; and it giveth light unto all that are in the house. Let your light so shine before men, that they may see your good works, and glorify your Father which is in heaven.

—Matthew 5:13–16

1483. When God blesses you, sing *"Hallelujah"*, and sustain that note! Don't let the praise end too fast. Keep the praises going between blessings. The sound of one *"Hallelujah"* can draw the next blessing to you. You'll go from faith to faith, strength to strength, and glory to glory!

Blessed be the Lord, who daily loadeth us with benefits, even the God of our salvation. Selah.

—Psalm 68:19

1484. It may taste good, but you must always consider the inevitable heartburn of partaking of the forbidden fruit of bad decisions.

And the Lord God took the man, and put him into the garden of Eden to dress it and to keep it. And the Lord God commanded the man, saying, Of every tree of the garden thou mayest freely eat: But of the tree of the knowledge of good and evil, thou shalt not eat of it: for in the day that thou eatest thereof thou shalt surely die.

—Genesis 2:15–17

1485. When you spend your life *running scared* about the bills, family, job, and world affairs, it's good to take a day to stop and let God restore your soul. Take time for rest and recreation in God's refuge for your soul.

The Lord is my shepherd; I shall not want. He maketh me to lie down in green pastures: he leadeth me beside the still waters. He restoreth my soul: he leadeth me in the paths of righteousness for his name's sake.

—Psalm 23:1–3

God is our refuge and strength, a very present help in trouble.

—Psalm 46:1

1486. No matter what difficulties you may be facing, today, know that God is always there with you. Rely on Him. He will bring you through. Know for sure that it is well with your soul.

God is our refuge and strength, a very present help in trouble.

—Psalm 46:1

1487. In times of confusion and transition, we must look to the light of God's presence and love. We must trust that He will always surround us and bring us through to the other side of the transition.

And the Lord said unto Moses, Stretch out thine hand toward heaven, that there may be darkness over the land of Egypt, even darkness which may be felt. And Moses stretched forth his hand toward heaven; and there was a thick darkness in all the land of Egypt three days: They saw not one another, neither rose any from his place for three days: but all the children of Israel had light in their dwellings.

—Exodus 10:21–23

1488. In spite of the conditions of the world in which we live, you can call on Jesus. You are invited into the world in which "we", the saints of God, live! Whosoever calls upon the name of the Lord shall be saved!

For God so loved the world, that he gave his only begotten Son, that whosoever believeth in him should not perish, but have everlasting life. For God sent not his Son into the world to condemn the world; but that the world through him might be saved.

—John 3:16–17

For whosoever shall call upon the name of the Lord shall be saved.

—Romans 10:13

1489. People who have what others don't have were willing to do what others weren't willing to do.

The crown of the wise is their riches: but the foolishness of fools is folly.

—Proverbs 14:24

1490. Make suggestions, not complaints.

And Pharaoh said unto Joseph, I have dreamed a dream, and there is none that can interpret it: and I have heard say of thee, that thou canst understand a dream to interpret it. And Joseph answered Pharaoh, saying, It is not in me: God shall give Pharaoh an answer of peace. And Pharaoh said unto Joseph, In my dream, behold, I stood upon the bank of the river: And, behold, there came up out of the river seven kine, fatfleshed and well favoured; and they fed in a meadow: And, behold, seven other kine came up after them, poor and very ill

favoured and leanfleshed, such as I never saw in all the land of Egypt for badness: And the lean and the ill favoured kine did eat up the first seven fat kine: And when they had eaten them up, it could not be known that they had eaten them; but they were still ill favoured, as at the beginning. So I awoke. And I saw in my dream, and, behold, seven ears came up in one stalk, full and good: And, behold, seven ears, withered, thin, and blasted with the east wind, sprung up after them: And the thin ears devoured the seven good ears: and I told this unto the magicians; but there was none that could declare it to me. And Joseph said unto Pharaoh, The dream of Pharaoh is one: God hath shewed Pharaoh what he is about to do. The seven good kine are seven years; and the seven good ears are seven years: the dream is one. And the seven thin and ill favoured kine that came up after them are seven years; and the seven empty ears blasted with the east wind shall be seven years of famine. This is the thing which I have spoken unto Pharaoh: What God is about to do he sheweth unto Pharaoh. Behold, there come seven years of great plenty throughout all the land of Egypt: And there shall arise after them seven years of famine; and all the plenty shall be forgotten in the land of Egypt; and the famine shall consume the land; And the plenty shall not be known in the land by reason of that famine following; for it shall be very grievous. And for that the dream was doubled unto Pharaoh twice; it is because the thing is established by God, and God will shortly bring it to pass. Now therefore let Pharaoh look out a man discreet and wise, and set him over the land of Egypt. Let Pharaoh do this, and let him appoint officers over the land, and take up the fifth part of the land of Egypt in the seven plenteous years. And let them gather all the food of those good years that come, and

lay up corn under the hand of Pharaoh, and let them keep food in the cities. And that food shall be for store to the land against the seven years of famine, which shall be in the land of Egypt; that the land perish not through the famine. And the thing was good in the eyes of Pharaoh, and in the eyes of all his servants. And Pharaoh said unto his servants, Can we find such a one as this is, a man in whom the Spirit of God is? And Pharaoh said unto Joseph, Forasmuch as God hath shewed thee all this, there is none so discreet and wise as thou art: Thou shalt be over my house, and according unto thy word shall all my people be ruled: only in the throne will I be greater than thou. And Pharaoh said unto Joseph, See, I have set thee over all the land of Egypt. And Pharaoh took off his ring from his hand, and put it upon Joseph's hand, and arrayed him in vestures of fine linen, and put a gold chain about his neck; And he made him to ride in the second chariot which he had; and they cried before him, Bow the knee: and he made him ruler over all the land of Egypt. And Pharaoh said unto Joseph, I am Pharaoh, and without thee shall no man lift up his hand or foot in all the land of Egypt. And Pharaoh called Joseph's name Zaphnathpaaneah; and he gave him to wife Asenath the daughter of Potipherah priest of On. And Joseph went out over all the land of Egypt. And Joseph was thirty years old when he stood before Pharaoh king of Egypt. And Joseph went out from the presence of Pharaoh, and went throughout all the land of Egypt.

—Genesis 41:15–46

1491. One of the ways to bring light back into the world, is to be nice to each person, one person at a time.

Pastor Terrance Levise Turner, MBA

Ye are the salt of the earth: but if the salt have lost his savour, wherewith shall it be salted? it is thenceforth good for nothing, but to be cast out, and to be trodden under foot of men. Ye are the light of the world. A city that is set on an hill cannot be hid. Neither do men light a candle, and put it under a bushel, but on a candlestick; and it giveth light unto all that are in the house. Let your light so shine before men, that they may see your good works, and glorify your Father which is in heaven.

—Matthew 5:13–16

1492. There's victory in faithfulness.

For whatsoever is born of God overcometh the world: and this is the victory that overcometh the world, even our faith.

—1 John 5:4

1493. Seek God for that one thing that you can do better than the average "Joe". Then, focus on becoming better and better at it. Refine yourself in it. Learn all you can about it. Then, commit to being the best at it. It will become your source of wealth, happiness, and contribution. It all starts with seeking God, your Heavenly Father, through prayer and studying The Bible, for guidance.

If any of you lack wisdom, let him ask of God, that giveth to all men liberally, and upbraideth not; and it shall be given him.

—James 1:5

1494. Seek God in praise and worship until you enter His higher realm. In His presence is fullness of joy! Your cares will begin to fall away, and answers will begin to enter your born-again spirit. You will gain strength for your journey, and you will gain the wisdom to obtain the blessing of the inheritance He has laid up for you. Praise and worship causes you to transcend the limited realm of the flesh, and you will then enter the realm of God's holy throne!

For thus saith the high and lofty One that inhabiteth eternity, whose name is Holy; I dwell in the high and holy place, with him also that is of a contrite and humble spirit, to revive the spirit of the humble, and to revive the heart of the contrite ones.

—Isaiah 57:15

1495. Future–oriented thought, plus a commitment to reach it, is the key to happiness, success, and abounding energy!

Where there is no vision, the people perish: but he that keepeth the law, happy is he.

—Proverbs 29:18

For a dream cometh through the multitude of business; and a fool's voice is known by multitude of words.

—Ecclesiastes 5:3

1496. Life is a portrait of moments. Take time to appreciate the picture that God has designed for you to enjoy. Enjoy the people that are in your life. Enjoy the times that you have set aside to enjoy one another. Life is a portrait of moments. Enjoy the beautiful picture God has given you!

He hath made every thing beautiful in his time: also he hath set the world in their heart, so that no man can find out the work that God maketh from the beginning to the end.

—Ecclesiastes 3:11

1497. Stay sober. Stay vigilant. Don't be so happy that you are not watchful. Don't be blindsided. Be effective and efficient. Have a great day.

Be sober, be vigilant; because your adversary the devil, as a roaring lion, walketh about, seeking whom he may devour: Whom resist stedfast in the faith, knowing that the same afflictions are accomplished in your brethren that are in the world.

−1 Peter 5:8–9

1498. When you set big goals, you always achieve more than you would have if you had no goals or low goals. Always set big goals. They will stretch your faith!

And they said, Go to, let us build us a city and a tower, whose top may reach unto heaven; and let us make us a name, lest we be scattered abroad upon the face of the whole earth. And the

Lord came down to see the city and the tower, which the children of men builded. And the Lord said, Behold, the people is one, and they have all one language; and this they begin to do: and now nothing will be restrained from them, which they have imagined to do.

—Genesis 11:4–6

1499. Avoid prestige events. They usually only make a lot of noise, but do little to positively affect the bottom-line. Only invest in events, people, and places that have real buyers of your value. Only go where you will be compensated.

In all labour there is profit: but the talk of the lips tendeth only to penury.

—Proverbs 14:23

1500. Jesus revealed the tactics and nature of the enemy, Satan, when He declared, "*the thief comes not, but for to steal, kill, and to destroy*". Don't think it strange if you see sudden "*fiery darts*" of trouble coming at you when there is something good happening in your life. That's just the schemes of the Devil to distract you from enjoying and embracing your blessings. Submit yourself to God in prayer, and resist the Devil, and he will flee from you. Then, enjoy your blessings, because you've got the victory, and there's nothing the enemy can do to take it!

Pastor Terrance Levise Turner, MBA

The thief cometh not, but for to steal, and to kill, and to destroy: I am come that they might have life, and that they might have it more abundantly.

—John 10:10

Beloved, think it not strange concerning the fiery trial which is to try you, as though some strange thing happened unto you.

–1 Peter 4:12

Above all, taking the shield of faith, wherewith ye shall be able to quench all the fiery darts of the wicked.

—Ephesians 6:16

Submit yourselves therefore to God. Resist the devil, and he will flee from you.

—James 4:7

Humble yourselves therefore under the mighty hand of God, that he may exalt you in due time: Casting all your care upon him; for he careth for you. Be sober, be vigilant; because your adversary the devil, as a roaring lion, walketh about, seeking whom he may devour: Whom resist stedfast in the faith, knowing that the same afflictions are accomplished in your brethren that are in the world.

–1 Peter 5:6–9

1501. What's in your heart should be in your actions.

—Hugo Nathaniel Walters

Even so faith, if it hath not works, is dead, being alone. Yea, a man may say, Thou hast faith, and I have works: shew me thy faith without thy works, and I will shew thee my faith by my works.

—James 2:17–18

1502. If your blessing is taking a long time, and it seems like your miracle is not coming as fast as you want, it's because God is teaching you to live by His principles, and not just by miracles. Principles work all the time. Miracles happen occasionally. It's God's favor to you to make you learn His principles. It's a sign of maturity, and the key to long-term security.

Hear, O my son, and receive my sayings; and the years of thy life shall be many. I have taught thee in the way of wisdom; I have led thee in right paths. When thou goest, thy steps shall not be straitened; and when thou runnest, thou shalt not stumble. Take fast hold of instruction; let her not go: keep her; for she is thy life.

—Proverbs 4:10–13

I love them that love me; and those that seek me early shall find me. Riches and honour are with me; yea, durable riches and righteousness. My fruit is better than gold, yea, than fine gold; and my revenue than choice silver. I lead in the way of righteousness, in the midst of the paths of judgment: That I

may cause those that love me to inherit substance; and I will fill their treasures.

—Proverbs 8:17–21

1503. There's never any draw back to being an *overachiever*. God wishes above all things that we prosper and be in health, even as our souls prosper. We should strive to exceed His expectations. No one will be mad, but your haters!

And Saul said, Thus shall ye say to David, The king desireth not any dowry, but an hundred foreskins of the Philistines, to be avenged of the king's enemies. But Saul thought to make David fall by the hand of the Philistines. And when his servants told David these words, it pleased David well to be the king's son in law: and the days were not expired. Wherefore David arose and went, he and his men, and slew of the Philistines two hundred men; and David brought their foreskins, and they gave them in full tale to the king, that he might be the king's son in law. And Saul gave him Michal his daughter to wife. And Saul saw and knew that the Lord was with David, and that Michal Saul's daughter loved him. And Saul was yet the more afraid of David; and Saul became David's enemy continually. Then the princes of the Philistines went forth: and it came to pass, after they went forth, that David behaved himself more wisely than all the servants of Saul; so that his name was much set by.

—1 Samuel 18:25–30

1504. To say "God is working on our behalf" is not a light thing or a trite thing. It's the *real thing*. Most people focus on their problems, like they're the real thing. But, problems are temporary. Yet, God's goodness is everlasting. Trust in God. His love and power is everlasting.

For his anger endureth but a moment; in his favour is life: weeping may endure for a night, but joy cometh in the morning.

—Psalm 30:5

1505. It's good to make a *splash* in life, because you never know how far the ripples will go!

And he came to Nazareth, where he had been brought up: and, as his custom was, he went into the synagogue on the sabbath day, and stood up for to read. And there was delivered unto him the book of the prophet Esaias. And when he had opened the book, he found the place where it was written, The Spirit of the Lord is upon me, because he hath anointed me to preach the gospel to the poor; he hath sent me to heal the brokenhearted, to preach deliverance to the captives, and recovering of sight to the blind, to set at liberty them that are bruised, To preach the acceptable year of the Lord. And he closed the book, and he gave it again to the minister, and sat down. And the eyes of all them that were in the synagogue were fastened on him. And he began to say unto them, This day is this scripture fulfilled in your ears. And all bare him witness, and wondered at the gracious words which

proceeded out of his mouth. And they said, Is not this Joseph's son?

—Luke 4:16–22

1506. When given a choice, always call *"heads!"* You always have a choice!

And the Lord shall make thee the head, and not the tail; and thou shalt be above only, and thou shalt not be beneath; if that thou hearken unto the commandments of the Lord thy God, which I command thee this day, to observe and to do them.

—Deuteronomy 28:13

I call heaven and earth to record this day against you, that I have set before you life and death, blessing and cursing: therefore choose life, that both thou and thy seed may live.

—Deuteronomy 30:19

1507. Don't wait until the battle is over: succeed now! Get something in your *back pocket* that you can be working on while you are walking toward your miracle and waiting on The Lord. Start that small business. Go back to school. Develop a profitable hobby. You will meet your miracle coming up the other side of the mountain. It will meet you at the right place and right time, in the place of destiny!

And that ye study to be quiet, and to do your own business, and to work with your own hands, as we commanded you;

that ye may walk honestly toward them that are without, and that ye may have lack of nothing.

–1 Thessalonians 4:11–12

1508. Jump-start your day with a song of praise! Recognize God as the author of your new day! Give Him thanksgiving for blessing you in all your ways. Jump-start each day with a song of praise! God deserves it, and you will feel better. Don't leave any room for complaining at the beginning of the day. Just start the morning with simple, sincere praise. You are inviting God's comfort and wisdom into your day!

It is a good thing to give thanks unto the Lord, and to sing praises unto thy name, O Most High: To shew forth thy lovingkindness in the morning, and thy faithfulness every night.

—Psalm 92:1–2

1509. Seek to please The Lord Jesus Christ today in all that you do. He's your source of reward and promotion in life. Treat others right, and work excellently. You will gain favor, goodwill, reward, good health, and promotion.

He that diligently seeketh good procureth favour: but he that seeketh mischief, it shall come unto him.

—Proverbs 11:27

For promotion cometh neither from the east, nor from the west, nor from the south. But God is the judge: he putteth down one, and setteth up another.

—Psalm 75:6–7

And whatsoever ye do, do it heartily, as to the Lord, and not unto men; knowing that of the Lord ye shall receive the reward of the inheritance: for ye serve the Lord Christ.

—Colossians 3:23–24

1510. When faced with the question of whether to take a positive opportunity or not, always take a chance!

Whatsoever thy hand findeth to do, do it with thy might; for there is no work, nor device, nor knowledge, nor wisdom, in the grave, whither thou goest. I returned, and saw under the sun, that the race is not to the swift, nor the battle to the strong, neither yet bread to the wise, nor yet riches to men of understanding, nor yet favour to men of skill; but time and chance happeneth to them all.

—Ecclesiastes 9:10–11

And there were four leprous men at the entering in of the gate: and they said one to another, Why sit we here until we die? If we say, We will enter into the city, then the famine is in the city, and we shall die there: and if we sit still here, we die also. Now therefore come, and let us fall unto the host of the Syrians: if they save us alive, we shall live; and if they kill us, we shall but die. And they rose up in the twilight, to go

Distinguished Wisdom Presents . . . "Living Proverbs"–Vol.3

unto the camp of the Syrians: and when they were come to the uttermost part of the camp of Syria, behold, there was no man there. For the Lord had made the host of the Syrians to hear a noise of chariots, and a noise of horses, even the noise of a great host: and they said one to another, Lo, the king of Israel hath hired against us the kings of the Hittites, and the kings of the Egyptians, to come upon us. Wherefore they arose and fled in the twilight, and left their tents, and their horses, and their asses, even the camp as it was, and fled for their life. And when these lepers came to the uttermost part of the camp, they went into one tent, and did eat and drink, and carried thence silver, and gold, and raiment, and went and hid it; and came again, and entered into another tent, and carried thence also, and went and hid it. Then they said one to another, We do not well: this day is a day of good tidings, and we hold our peace: if we tarry till the morning light, some mischief will come upon us: now therefore come, that we may go and tell the king's household. So they came and called unto the porter of the city: and they told them, saying, We came to the camp of the Syrians, and, behold, there was no man there, neither voice of man, but horses tied, and asses tied, and the tents as they were. And he called the porters; and they told it to the king's house within. And the king arose in the night, and said unto his servants, I will now shew you what the Syrians have done to us. They know that we be hungry; therefore are they gone out of the camp to hide themselves in the field, saying, When they come out of the city, we shall catch them alive, and get into the city. And one of his servants answered and said, Let some take, I pray thee, five of the horses that remain, which are left in the city, (behold, they are as all the multitude of Israel that are left in it: behold, I say,

they are even as all the multitude of the Israelites that are consumed:) and let us send and see. They took therefore two chariot horses; and the king sent after the host of the Syrians, saying, Go and see. And they went after them unto Jordan: and, lo, all the way was full of garments and vessels, which the Syrians had cast away in their haste. And the messengers returned, and told the king. And the people went out, and spoiled the tents of the Syrians. So a measure of fine flour was sold for a shekel, and two measures of barley for a shekel, according to the Word of the Lord. And the king appointed the Lord on whose hand he leaned to have the charge of the gate: and the people trode upon him in the gate, and he died, as the man of God had said, who spake when the king came down to him. And it came to pass as the man of God had spoken to the king, saying, Two measures of barley for a shekel, and a measure of fine flour for a shekel, shall be to morrow about this time in the gate of Samaria: And that lord answered the man of God, and said, Now, behold, if the Lord should make windows in heaven, might such a thing be? And he said, Behold, thou shalt see it with thine eyes, but shalt not eat thereof. And so it fell out unto him: for the people trode upon him in the gate, and he died.

−2 Kings 7:3–20

1511. Change your feelings with an act.

Beat your plowshares into swords and your pruninghooks into spears: let the weak say, I am strong.

—Joel 3:10

Have not I commanded thee? Be strong and of a good courage; be not afraid, neither be thou dismayed: for the Lord thy God is with thee whithersoever thou goest.

—Joshua 1:9

1512. Let excellence be the signature of your work today. Show people who you are by what you do and the attitude you do it in. Represent the high standards of God in all that you do. You are a child of The Most High God.

And over these three presidents; of whom Daniel was first: that the princes might give accounts unto them, and the king should have no damage. Then this Daniel was preferred above the presidents and princes, because an excellent spirit was in him; and the king thought to set him over the whole realm. Then the presidents and princes sought to find occasion against Daniel concerning the kingdom; but they could find none occasion nor fault; forasmuch as he was faithful, neither was there any error or fault found in him.

—Daniel 6:2–4

1513. As you and I come to the end of each day, let us always take time to seek God for His wisdom and insight for our lives. Get wisdom and get understanding, by taking time to study, research, practice, and pray.

Through desire a man, having separated himself, seeketh and intermeddleth with all wisdom.

—Proverbs 18:1

1514. Prayer-time is power-time! Anytime you take time to pray, you hook-up to the power of God. Start the day in prayer. You'll find the power of God for your day!

And in the morning, rising up a great while before day, he went out, and departed into a solitary place, and there prayed.

—Mark 1:35

1515. Celebrating Black History

And the whole earth was of one language, and of one speech. And it came to pass, as they journeyed from the east, that they found a plain in the land of Shinar; and they dwelt there. And they said one to another, Go to, let us make brick, and burn them thoroughly. And they had brick for stone, and slime had they for morter. And they said, Go to, let us build us a city and a tower, whose top may reach unto heaven; and let us make us a name, lest we be scattered abroad upon the face of the whole earth. And the Lord came down to see the city and the tower, which the children of men builded. And the Lord said, Behold, the people is one, and they have all one language; and this they begin to do: and now nothing will be restrained from them, which they have imagined to do. Go to, let us go down, and there confound their language, that they may not understand one another's speech. So the Lord scattered them abroad from thence upon the face of all the earth: and they left off to build the city. Therefore is the name of it called Babel; because the Lord did there confound the language of all the earth: and from thence did the Lord scatter them abroad upon the face of all the earth.

—Genesis 11:1-9

For as I passed by, and beheld your devotions, I found an altar with this inscription, To The Unknown God. Whom therefore ye ignorantly worship, him declare I unto you. God that made the world and all things therein, seeing that he is Lord of heaven and earth, dwelleth not in temples made with hands; Neither is worshipped with men's hands, as though he needed any thing, seeing he giveth to all life, and breath, and all things; And hath made of one blood all nations of men for to dwell on all the face of the earth, and hath determined the times before appointed, and the bounds of their habitation; That they should seek the Lord, if haply they might feel after him, and find him, though he be not far from every one of us: For in him we live, and move, and have our being; as certain also of your own poets have said, For we are also his offspring.

—Acts 17:23-28

1516. Success is process oriented.

The steps of a good man are ordered by the Lord: and he delighteth in his way.

—Psalm 37:23

1517. I'm into the Bible, and the Bible is into me, and that's where it needs to be!

Abide in me, and I in you. As the branch cannot bear fruit of itself, except it abide in the vine; no more can ye, except ye abide in me. I am the vine, ye are the branches: He that

abideth in me, and I in him, the same bringeth forth much fruit: for without me ye can do nothing. If a man abide not in me, he is cast forth as a branch, and is withered; and men gather them, and cast them into the fire, and they are burned. If ye abide in me, and my words abide in you, ye shall ask what ye will, and it shall be done unto you.

—John 15:4–7

1518. The very fact that hundreds of thousands, and even millions of people have gone from the bottom to the top in every field is ample proof that you can do it as well.

—Brian Tracy

— (From the book *Goals!*)

Seest thou a man diligent in his business? he shall stand before kings; he shall not stand before mean men.

—Proverbs 22:29

1519. In most areas of life, it is more hard work and dedication, than natural ability and talent that lead to excellence and success.

—Brian Tracy

—(From the book *Goals!*)

Seest thou a man diligent in his business? he shall stand before kings; he shall not stand before mean men.

—Proverbs 22:29

1520. May your life be fulfilled by all of the exceedingly great and precious promises of God. May your life legacy be a lasting monument of all of God's promises having been fulfilled. In Jesus name, amen.

Whereby are given unto us exceeding great and precious promises: that by these ye might be partakers of the divine nature, having escaped the corruption that is in the world through lust.

—2 Peter 1:4

Praise ye the Lord. Blessed is the man that feareth the Lord, that delighteth greatly in his commandments. His seed shall be mighty upon earth: the generation of the upright shall be blessed. Wealth and riches shall be in his house: and his righteousness endureth for ever. Unto the upright there ariseth light in the darkness: he is gracious, and full of compassion, and righteous. A good man sheweth favour, and lendeth: he will guide his affairs with discretion. Surely he shall not be moved for ever: the righteous shall be in everlasting remembrance. He shall not be afraid of evil tidings: his heart is fixed, trusting in the Lord. His heart is established, he shall not be afraid, until he see his desire upon his enemies. He hath dispersed, he hath given to the poor; his righteousness endureth for ever; his horn shall be exalted with honour. The wicked shall see it, and be grieved; he shall gnash with his teeth, and melt away: the desire of the wicked shall perish.

—Psalm 112

Mark the perfect man, and behold the upright: for the end of that man is peace.

—Psalm 37:37

1521. Take time to read, study, and research; and thus, avoid paying the *"fool's fee"* of ignorance or exorbitant prices for what's readily available to all!

Also, that the soul be without knowledge, it is not good; and he that hasteth with his feet sinneth.

—Proverbs 19:2

1522. Thank God today for a new beginning! This is an opportunity to use the energy and life you have renewed this weekend, and choose to have an outstanding new week! You have the power to choose victory or defeat, joy or sadness, self–pity or gladness. Choose life this week, and have a victorious week!

Blessed be the Lord, who daily loadeth us with benefits, even the God of our salvation. Selah.

—Psalm 68:19

1523. Use every vehicle necessary to accelerate your progress on the journey of life. Even though the waves may be boisterous, you can power through in the vehicle of

acceleration! Every important journey or mission needs a vehicle of acceleration. Education, training, mentors, and workshops are all vehicles for accelerating your destiny!

And it came to pass, that, as the people pressed upon him to hear the Word of God, he stood by the lake of Gennesaret, And saw two ships standing by the lake: but the fishermen were gone out of them, and were washing their nets. And he entered into one of the ships, which was Simon's, and prayed him that he would thrust out a little from the land. And he sat down, and taught the people out of the ship. Now when he had left speaking, he said unto Simon, Launch out into the deep, and let down your nets for a draught. And Simon answering said unto him, Master, we have toiled all the night, and have taken nothing: nevertheless at thy word I will let down the net. And when they had this done, they inclosed a great multitude of fishes: and their net brake. And they beckoned unto their partners, which were in the other ship, that they should come and help them. And they came, and filled both the ships, so that they began to sink. When Simon Peter saw it, he fell down at Jesus' knees, saying, Depart from me; for I am a sinful man, O Lord. For he was astonished, and all that were with him, at the draught of the fishes which they had taken: And so was also James, and John, the sons of Zebedee, which were partners with Simon. And Jesus said unto Simon, Fear not; from henceforth thou shalt catch men. And when they had brought their ships to land, they forsook all, and followed him.

—Luke 5:1–11

Pastor Terrance Levise Turner, MBA

1524. I declare and decree a statistically measurable increase of relationships between eligible men and women, leading to traditional marriages between one man and one woman, and a measurable increase of healthy, happy children born into those marriages over the next 10–15 years; and a statistically measurable increase of wealth and income among existing traditionally married men and women over the next 10–15 years. In Jesus name, amen.

Blessed is every one that feareth the Lord; that walketh in his ways. For thou shalt eat the labour of thine hands: happy shalt thou be, and it shall be well with thee. Thy wife shall be as a fruitful vine by the sides of thine house: thy children like olive plants round about thy table. Behold, that thus shall the man be blessed that feareth the Lord. The Lord shall bless thee out of Zion: and thou shalt see the good of Jerusalem all the days of thy life. Yea, thou shalt see thy children's children, and peace upon Israel.

—Psalm 128

1525. The more you know the less you should have to pay, because you know better.

Also, that the soul be without knowledge, it is not good; and he that hasteth with his feet sinneth.

—Proverbs 19:2

It is naught, it is naught, saith the buyer: but when he is gone his way, then he boasteth.

—Proverbs 20:14

Wisdom is good with an inheritance: and by it there is profit to them that see the sun. For wisdom is a defence, and money is a defence: but the excellency of knowledge is, that wisdom giveth life to them that have it.

—Ecclesiastes 7:11–12

1526. Consider the ant and be wise. Even an ant can build themselves a suitable home with the *sands of time*, which we waste each day. Maximize each moment. Invest in the future. Prepare for tomorrow. Enjoy today.

There be four things which are little upon the earth, but they are exceeding wise: The ants are a people not strong, yet they prepare their meat in the summer.

—Proverbs 30:24–25

Go to the ant, thou sluggard; consider her ways, and be wise: which having no guide, overseer, or ruler, provideth her meat in the summer, and gathereth her food in the harvest.

—Proverbs 6:6–8

1527. Rather than allowing your happiness to fluctuate from happening to happening, choose to rejoice in The Lord always, based on the abiding joy of your salvation from sin, and the indwelling embrace of Christ's life and life more abundantly!

Rejoice in the Lord always: and again I say, Rejoice. Let your moderation be known unto all men. The Lord is at hand. Be careful for nothing; but in every thing by prayer and supplication with thanksgiving let your requests be made known unto God. And the peace of God, which passeth all understanding, shall keep your hearts and minds through Christ Jesus. Finally, brethren, whatsoever things are true, whatsoever things are honest, whatsoever things are just, whatsoever things are pure, whatsoever things are lovely, whatsoever things are of good report; if there be any virtue, and if there be any praise, think on these things. Those things, which ye have both learned, and received, and heard, and seen in me, do: and the God of peace shall be with you.

—Philippians 4:4–9

1528. Poverty is what kills. Jesus and money is what heals. The un–regenerate spirit, the un–renewed mind, and the lack of money is at the root of most of the tragic, wasteful experiences in our families and communities. We must be born–again, renew our minds to God's principles, and work diligently to obtain wealth in order to curtail the pandemic effects of poverty.

The Spirit of the Lord is upon me, because he hath anointed me to preach the gospel to the poor; he hath sent me to heal the brokenhearted, to preach deliverance to the captives, and recovering of sight to the blind, to set at liberty them that are bruised, To preach the acceptable year of the Lord.

—Luke 4:18–19

1529. A wife is a gift from God. She is a treasure to enrich the life of her husband for a lifetime. Husbands are entrusted with the value and beauty of her worth. May all marriages between godly men and women be prosperous, flourish and endure into a glorious future legacy. May your home bring continuous glory to God, your Heavenly Father. In Jesus name, amen.

Who can find a virtuous woman? for her price is far above rubies. The heart of her husband doth safely trust in her, so that he shall have no need of spoil. She will do him good and not evil all the days of her life.

—Proverbs 31:10–12

1530. You can't play games with someone who has already won.

And in nothing terrified by your adversaries: which is to them an evident token of perdition, but to you of salvation, and that of God.

—Proverbs 18:22

1531. Confrontation is a part of healthy relationships. A relationship completely absent of occasional confrontation is indicative of hypocrisy or the presence of fear.

But speaking the truth in love, may grow up into him in all things, which is the head, *even* Christ.

—Ephesians 4:15

There is no fear in love; but perfect love casteth out fear: because fear hath torment. He that feareth is not made perfect in love.

−1 John 4:18

1532. Discretion is the key to long-term relationships with honorable people. Discretion can invite you in, and indiscretion can invite you out!

The proverbs of Solomon the son of David, king of Israel; To know wisdom and instruction; to perceive the Words of understanding; To receive the instruction of wisdom, justice, and judgment, and equity; To give subtilty to the simple, to the young man knowledge and discretion. A wise man will hear, and will increase learning; and a man of understanding shall attain unto wise counsels.

—Proverbs 1:1–5

As a jewel of gold in a swine's snout, so is a fair woman which is without discretion.

—Proverbs 11:22

1533. It's one thing to say, *"And it's coming to pass"*. It's another thing to say, *"I'm bringing it to pass"*. One depends on blind faith. The other depends on personal responsibility. You still have to depend on God. Yet, you have developed the

wisdom of knowing that nothing just happens without our personal commitment and participation.

Even so faith, if it hath not works, is dead, being alone. Yea, a man may say, Thou hast faith, and I have works: shew me thy faith without thy works, and I will shew thee my faith by my works.

—James 2:17–18

1534. There is an exercise of faith whereby you get just what you say. As we continue to develop in this faith, we will become stronger and stronger, and reach a new level and a new dimension of faith and authority in the earth. As we decree, declare, and command a desired outcome, with no doubt, we will begin to exercise our birthright.

And Jesus answering saith unto them, Have faith in God. For verily I say unto you, That whosoever shall say unto this mountain, Be thou removed, and be thou cast into the sea; and shall not doubt in his heart, but shall believe that those things which he saith shall come to pass; he shall have whatsoever he saith. Therefore I say unto you, What things soever ye desire, when ye pray, believe that ye receive them, and ye shall have them.

—Mark 11:22–24

1535. It's a paradisiacal day! Paradisiacal is defined, *of, like, or befitting paradise*. It's always paradise when God is in the

midst! He will keep you in perfect peace when your mind is stayed on Him!

These are the generations of the heavens and of the earth when they were created, in the day that the Lord God made the earth and the heavens, And every plant of the field before it was in the earth, and every herb of the field before it grew: for the Lord God had not caused it to rain upon the earth, and there was not a man to till the ground. But there went up a mist from the earth, and watered the whole face of the ground. And the Lord God formed man of the dust of the ground, and breathed into his nostrils the breath of life; and man became a living soul. And the Lord God planted a garden eastward in Eden; and there he put the man whom he had formed. And out of the ground made the Lord God to grow every tree that is pleasant to the sight, and good for food; the tree of life also in the midst of the garden, and the tree of knowledge of good and evil. And a river went out of Eden to water the garden; and from thence it was parted, and became into four heads. The name of the first is Pison: that is it which compasseth the whole land of Havilah, where there is gold; And the gold of that land is good: there is bdellium and the onyx stone. And the name of the second river is Gihon: the same is it that compasseth the whole land of Ethiopia. And the name of the third river is Hiddekel: that is it which goeth toward the east of Assyria. And the fourth river is Euphrates. And the Lord God took the man, and put him into the garden of Eden to dress it and to keep it.

—Genesis 2:4–15

1536. Marriages made in Heaven are worked out on Earth.

Wives, submit yourselves unto your own husbands, as unto the Lord. For the husband is the head of the wife, even as Christ is the head of the church: and he is the saviour of the body. Therefore as the church is subject unto Christ, so let the wives be to their own husbands in every thing. Husbands, love your wives, even as Christ also loved the church, and gave himself for it; That he might sanctify and cleanse it with the washing of water by the Word, That he might present it to himself a glorious church, not having spot, or wrinkle, or any such thing; but that it should be holy and without blemish. So ought men to love their wives as their own bodies. He that loveth his wife loveth himself. For no man ever yet hated his own flesh; but nourisheth and cherisheth it, even as the Lord the church: For we are members of his body, of his flesh, and of his bones. For this cause shall a man leave his father and mother, and shall be joined unto his wife, and they two shall be one flesh. This is a great mystery: but I speak concerning Christ and the church. Nevertheless let every one of you in particular so love his wife even as himself; and the wife see that she reverence her husband.

—Ephesians 5:22–33

1537. People who can't improve you shouldn't reprove you. Their information or opinion really doesn't matter.

Now as touching things offered unto idols, we know that we all have knowledge. Knowledge puffeth up, but charity edifieth.

–1 Corinthians 8:1

1538. Husbands and wives, if you are Christians, you should live your lives, and conduct your marriage according to the Bible's standard, and not according to secular society. Today's society is rebelling against God's standard for marriage, and male and female roles. However, God's plan works. It's the key to long-term happiness, peace, and success in marriage and family life.

Wives, submit yourselves unto your own husbands, as unto the Lord. For the husband is the head of the wife, even as Christ is the head of the church: and he is the saviour of the body. Therefore as the church is subject unto Christ, so let the wives be to their own husbands in every thing. Husbands, love your wives, even as Christ also loved the church, and gave himself for it; That he might sanctify and cleanse it with the washing of water by the Word, That he might present it to himself a glorious church, not having spot, or wrinkle, or any such thing; but that it should be holy and without blemish. So ought men to love their wives as their own bodies. He that loveth his wife loveth himself. For no man ever yet hated his own flesh; but nourisheth and cherisheth it, even as the Lord the church: For we are members of his body, of his flesh, and of his bones. For this cause shall a man leave his father and mother, and shall be joined unto his wife, and they two shall be one flesh. This is a great mystery: but I speak concerning Christ and the church. Nevertheless let every one of you in particular so love his wife even as himself; and the wife see that she reverence her husband.

—Ephesians 5:22–33

1539. Don't keep your niceness as a secret.

Ye are the salt of the earth: but if the salt have lost his savour, wherewith shall it be salted? it is thenceforth good for nothing, but to be cast out, and to be trodden under foot of men. Ye are the light of the world. A city that is set on an hill cannot be hid. Neither do men light a candle, and put it under a bushel, but on a candlestick; and it giveth light unto all that are in the house. Let your light so shine before men, that they may see your good works, and glorify your Father which is in heaven.

—Matthew 5:13–16

1540. One of the ways to overcome oppression is to oppress your oppressor with your peace.

And Jesus stood before the governor: and the governor asked him, saying, Art thou the King of the Jews? And Jesus said unto him, Thou sayest. And when he was accused of the chief priests and elders, he answered nothing. Then said Pilate unto him, Hearest thou not how many things they witness against thee? And he answered him to never a word; insomuch that the governor marvelled greatly.

—Matthew 27:11–14

1541. Regarding celebrating Black history, if it were not for the ones that fought back, the voices of the ones that were peaceful would not have been heard.

Wherefore seeing we also are compassed about with so great a cloud of witnesses, let us lay aside every weight, and the sin which doth so easily beset us, and let us run with patience the race that is set before us, Looking unto Jesus the author and finisher of our faith; who for the joy that was set before him endured the cross, despising the shame, and is set down at the right hand of the throne of God. For consider him that endured such contradiction of sinners against himself, lest ye be wearied and faint in your minds. Ye have not yet resisted unto blood, striving against sin.

—Hebrews 12:1–4

1542. Results come from hard, smart work. If you do what successful people do, you can have what successful people have.

Then Peter opened his mouth, and said, Of a truth I perceive that God is no respecter of persons: But in every nation he that feareth him, and worketh righteousness, is accepted with him.

—Acts 10:34–35

1543. You can't listen to losers about winning!

For a dream cometh through the multitude of business; and a fool's voice is known by multitude of words.

—Ecclesiastes 5:3

1544. An outstanding day starts with outstanding preparation. Take time in the morning to sing a song of thanksgiving, pray a prayer of faith, meditate a focus scripture, and confess a dynamic victory confession over your life! Have an awesome day!

That the communication of thy faith may become effectual by the acknowledging of every good thing which is in you in Christ Jesus.

—Philemon 1:6

1545. Everyday is a new opportunity to exceed the other! Do not be limited by your past or the opinions of others. Everyday is an opportunity to exceed the other!

Brethren, I count not myself to have apprehended: but this one thing I do, forgetting those things which are behind, and reaching forth unto those things which are before, I press toward the mark for the prize of the high calling of God in Christ Jesus.

—Philippians 3:13–14

1546. Upon the birth of a new idea, do not present it to a negative person, because they will damage your idea with

their negative opinion causing your *"baby"* to have a low self-image.

For who hath despised the day of small things? for they shall rejoice, and shall see the plummet in the hand of Zerubbabel with those seven; they are the eyes of the Lord, which run to and fro through the whole earth.

—Zechariah 4:10

1547. No matter what yesterday held for you, today is a new day. Choose to praise the Lord today for all the goodness He has in store for you. He has already been good to you. Be sure that the blessings will continue!

Bless the Lord, O my soul: and all that is within me, bless his holy name. Bless the Lord, O my soul, and forget not all his benefits.

—Psalm 103:1–2

1548. As you start each day, leave no space for the Devil. Leave no space of your life void of the Word of God. Speak the Word only!

Neither give place to the devil.

—Ephesians 4:27

The centurion answered and said, Lord, I am not worthy that thou shouldest come under my roof: but speak the Word only, and my servant shall be healed.

—Matthew 8:8

1549. Confidence is like jet fuel to the jet. We each have great equipment, yet we have to put forth effort to keep the fuel level full, in order to perform at our ultimate potential. Faith comes by hearing, and hearing by The Word of God. It is our source of true godly confidence.

So then faith cometh by hearing, and hearing by the Word of God.

—Romans 10:17

For I am not ashamed of the gospel of Christ: for it is the power of God unto salvation to every one that believeth; to the Jew first, and also to the Greek. For therein is the righteousness of God revealed from faith to faith: as it is written, The just shall live by faith.

—Romans 1:16–17

1550. As we have come to the end of the day, let us worship and praise the Lord Jesus Christ, the King of Kings and Lord of Lords. Worship His holiness. Adore His preciousness. And bask in His presence. He will heal your heart, calm your fears, and minister to your needs. Take time to tell Him that He's magnificent! You will be blessed.

The Lord is the portion of mine inheritance and of my cup: thou maintainest my lot. The lines are fallen unto me in pleasant places; yea, I have a goodly heritage. I will bless the Lord, who hath given me counsel: my reins also instruct me in

the night seasons. I have set the Lord always before me: because he is at my right hand, I shall not be moved. Therefore my heart is glad, and my glory rejoiceth: my flesh also shall rest in hope. For thou wilt not leave my soul in hell; neither wilt thou suffer thine Holy One to see corruption. Thou wilt shew me the path of life: in thy presence is fulness of joy; at thy right hand there are pleasures for evermore.

—Psalm 16:5–11

1551. A young man asked a wealthy, wise old woman, how long does it take to be successful? She answered, "A lifetime". You're not completely successful until you finish your race. You don't have true riches until you hear Jesus say, "Well done, good and faithful servant, you've been faithful over a few things, I will make you ruler over many things. Enter into the joy of your Lord". So keep striving everyday, until you have the eternal crown of the victorious *"finisher"* on your head!

The crown of the wise is their riches: but the foolishness of fools is folly.

—Proverbs 14:24

For the kingdom: of heaven is as a man travelling into a far country, who called his own servants, and delivered unto them his goods. And unto one he gave five talents, to another two, and to another one; to every man according to his several ability; and straightway took his journey. Then he that had received the five talents went and traded with the same, and

made them other five talents. And likewise he that had received two, he also gained other two. But he that had received one went and digged in the earth, and hid his lord's money. After a long time the Lord of those servants cometh, and reckoneth with them. And so he that had received five talents came and brought other five talents, saying, Lord, thou deliveredst unto me five talents: behold, I have gained beside them five talents more. His lord said unto him, Well done, thou good and faithful servant: thou hast been faithful over a few things, I will make thee ruler over many things: enter thou into the joy of thy lord. He also that had received two talents came and said, Lord, thou deliveredst unto me two talents: behold, I have gained two other talents beside them. His lord said unto him, Well done, good and faithful servant; thou hast been faithful over a few things, I will make thee ruler over many things: enter thou into the joy of thy lord.

—Matthew 25:14–23

1552. Value you. Always take care of yourself, because even if you don't feel like you're winning, you should always look like you're winning, and then when you look at yourself, you can simply say, "I'm winning!"

What shall we then say to these things? If God be for us, who can be against us? He that spared not his own Son, but delivered him up for us all, how shall he not with him also freely give us all things? Who shall lay any thing to the charge of God's elect? It is God that justifieth. Who is he that condemneth? It is Christ that died, yea rather, that is risen again, who is even at the right hand of God, who also maketh

intercession for us. Who shall separate us from the love of Christ? shall tribulation, or distress, or persecution, or famine, or nakedness, or peril, or sword? As it is written, For thy sake we are killed all the day long; we are accounted as sheep for the slaughter. Nay, in all these things we are more than conquerors through him that loved us. For I am persuaded, that neither death, nor life, nor angels, nor principalities, nor powers, nor things present, nor things to come, Nor height, nor depth, nor any other creature, shall be able to separate us from the love of God, which is in Christ Jesus our Lord.

—Romans 8:31–39

1553. Eagles fly higher!

But they that wait upon the Lord shall renew their strength; they shall mount up with wings as eagles; they shall run, and not be weary; and they shall walk, and not faint.

—Isaiah 40:31

1554. The key to success is love. Faith works by love. You must have a desire or hope for something better in order to use your faith to turn the key. However, the key to success is love. You must love others in order for God to open the door of your heart's desire to be released to you. It is *The Golden Rule*. It is "*The Royal Law*" on The King of Kings highway!

If ye fulfil the royal law according to the scripture, Thou shalt love thy neighbour as thyself, ye do well.

—James 2:8

1555. Concerning a harvest, it's work to prep the ground. It's work to plant the ground. It's work to tend the field. And, it's work to get in the harvest. Then, it's work to maintain the harvest. It's work! Work! Work! Work! Work! And it's worth it!

He that tilleth his land shall be satisfied with bread: but he that followeth vain persons is void of understanding.

—Proverbs 12:11

For a dream cometh through the multitude of business; and a fool's voice is known by multitude of words.

—Ecclesiastes 5:3

In the morning sow thy seed, and in the evening withhold not thine hand: for thou knowest not whether shall prosper, either this or that, or whether they both shall be alike good.

—Ecclesiastes 11:6

1556. As a person and a pastor, sometimes people don't want to hear your advice. They just want you to hear their problems. They then will consider your advice, but will still make the final decision for their life, because we're all sovereign in our own lives.

If thou be wise, thou shalt be wise for thyself: but if thou scornest, thou alone shalt bear it.

—Proverbs 9:12

1557. In every person's life, at some point there must be personal responsibility, and personal consequences.

Be not deceived; God is not mocked: for whatsoever a man soweth, that shall he also reap. For he that soweth to his flesh shall of the flesh reap corruption; but he that soweth to the Spirit shall of the Spirit reap life everlasting. And let us not be weary in well doing: for in due season we shall reap, if we faint not. As we have therefore opportunity, let us do good unto all men, especially unto them who are of the household of faith.

—Galatians 6:7–10

1558. If the current pond of possibility is too crowded for you to make a splash, create a new pond. Opportunity is always available. Even, if you have to cultivate it yourself.

But when it pleased God, who separated me from my mother's womb, and called me by his grace, to reveal his Son in me, that I might preach him among the heathen; immediately I conferred not with flesh and blood: neither went I up to Jerusalem to them which were apostles before me; but I went into Arabia, and returned again unto Damascus. Then after three years I went up to Jerusalem to see Peter, and abode with him fifteen days. But other of the apostles saw I none, save James the Lord's brother.

—Galatians 1:15–19

1559. Rather than living on a hope and a prayer, choose to develop a disciplined prayer-life.

And he spake a parable unto them to this end, that men ought always to pray, and not to faint; Saying, There was in a city a judge, which feared not God, neither regarded man: And there was a widow in that city; and she came unto him, saying, Avenge me of mine adversary. And he would not for a while: but afterward he said within himself, Though I fear not God, nor regard man; Yet because this widow troubleth me, I will avenge her, lest by her continual coming she weary me. And the Lord said, Hear what the unjust judge saith. And shall not God avenge his own elect, which cry day and night unto him, though he bear long with them? I tell you that he will avenge them speedily. Nevertheless when the Son of man cometh, shall he find faith on the earth?

—Luke 18:1–8

1560. We're all on this journey, trying to help one another along the way. There's no room for finger-pointing, and there's no room for condemnation.

There is therefore now no condemnation to them which are in Christ Jesus, who walk not after the flesh, but after the Spirit. For the law of the Spirit of life in Christ Jesus hath made me free from the law of sin and death.

—Romans 8:1–2

1561. Keep praising God for the blessing. Rebuke the Devil for his messing. Focus on praising God for what He's done and is doing for you. Drown out the lies of the Devil with your praise! Submit yourself unto God in worship. Resist the Devil, and he will flee from you!

Submit yourselves therefore to God. Resist the devil, and he will flee from you.

—James 4:7

1562. There are some people that *wither–up* early on the vine because of a sour attitude. Like raisins, they are headed to a *box* earlier than they should be. My advice: stay fresh all of your life, by maintaining the joyful juices of a positive attitude!

A merry heart doeth good like a medicine: but a broken spirit drieth the bones.

—Proverbs 17:22

1563. Contrary to popular belief, it doesn't take a crowd to succeed. It takes personal responsibility and personal commitment.

But let every man prove his own work, and then shall he have rejoicing in himself alone, and not in another.

—Galatians 6:4

1564. All work and no play makes you pull your hair out, become a wreck, or at least burn out! God created rest and recreation at the end of the work-week.

And he said unto them, Come ye yourselves apart into a desert place, and rest a while: for there were many coming and going, and they had no leisure so much as to eat.

—Mark 6:31

1565. There is power in singing songs of thanksgiving, praise, and worship to God, your Creator, because He is good. He opened your eyes this morning and let you see the beautiful sunshine. It is Him that protects you during the day. Praise Him! You will feel better!

It is a good thing to give thanks unto the Lord, and to sing praises unto thy name, O most High: to shew forth thy lovingkindness in the morning, and thy faithfulness every night.

—Psalm 92:1–2

1566. It's all about standing out. If you are outstanding, you should stand out!

Ye are the salt of the earth: but if the salt have lost his savour, wherewith shall it be salted? it is thenceforth good for nothing, but to be cast out, and to be trodden under foot of men. Ye are the light of the world. A city that is set on an hill cannot be hid. Neither do men light a candle, and put it under

a bushel, but on a candlestick; and it giveth light unto all that are in the house. Let your light so shine before men, that they may see your good works, and glorify your Father which is in heaven.

—Matthew 5:13–16

I have given them thy word; and the world hath hated them, because they are not of the world, even as I am not of the world. I pray not that thou shouldest take them out of the world, but that thou shouldest keep them from the evil. They are not of the world, even as I am not of the world. Sanctify them through thy truth: thy word is truth. As thou hast sent me into the world, even so have I also sent them into the world. And for their sakes I sanctify myself, that they also might be sanctified through the truth.

—John 17:14–19

1567. You don't have to fight for your right. When you're right, your right will fight for you.

The wicked flee when no man pursueth: but the righteous are bold as a lion.

—Proverbs 28:1

And in nothing terrified by your adversaries: which is to them an evident token of perdition, but to you of salvation, and that of God.

—Philippians 1:28

1568. Marriage is honorable, and the bed is undefiled; but whoremongers and adulterers God will judge. We should honor the marriage covenant between a man and a woman, and be faithful to our own spouses. Without faithfulness, husbands and wives violate and negate the force of their covenant, and cheat themselves out of the blessing upon their marriage.

I made a covenant with mine eyes; why then should I think upon a maid? For what portion of God is there from above? and what inheritance of the Almighty from on high? Is not destruction to the wicked? and a strange punishment to the workers of iniquity? Doth not he see my ways, and count all my steps? If I have walked with vanity, or if my foot hath hasted to deceit; Let me be weighed in an even balance that God may know mine integrity. If my step hath turned out of the way, and mine heart walked after mine eyes, and if any blot hath cleaved to mine hands; Then let me sow, and let another eat; yea, let my offspring be rooted out. If mine heart have been deceived by a woman, or if I have laid wait at my neighbour's door; Then let my wife grind unto another, and let others bow down upon her. For this is an heinous crime; yea, it is an iniquity to be punished by the judges. For it is a fire that consumeth to destruction, and would root out all mine increase.

—Job 31:1–12

For the commandment is a lamp; and the law is light; and reproofs of instruction are the way of life: To keep thee from the evil woman, from the flattery of the tongue of a strange

woman. Lust not after her beauty in thine heart; neither let her take thee with her eyelids. For by means of a whorish woman a man is brought to a piece of bread: and the adultress will hunt for the precious life. Can a man take fire in his bosom, and his clothes not be burned? Can one go upon hot coals, and his feet not be burned? So he that goeth in to his neighbour's wife; whosoever toucheth her shall not be innocent. Men do not despise a thief, if he steal to satisfy his soul when he is hungry; But if he be found, he shall restore sevenfold; he shall give all the substance of his house. But whoso committeth adultery with a woman lacketh understanding: he that doeth it destroyeth his own soul. A wound and dishonour shall he get; and his reproach shall not be wiped away. For jealousy is the rage of a man: therefore he will not spare in the day of vengeance. He will not regard any ransom; neither will he rest content, though thou givest many gifts.

—Proverbs 6:23–35

Marriage is honorable in all, and the bed undefiled: but whoremongers and adulterers God will judge.

—Hebrews 13:4

Whoso findeth a wife findeth a good thing, and obtaineth favour of the Lord.

—Proverbs 18:22

1569. Love your neighbor as you love yourself, but be sure to love yourself.

He that getteth wisdom loveth his own soul: he that keepeth understanding shall find good.

—Proverbs 19:8

Jesus said unto him, Thou shalt love the Lord thy God with all thy heart, and with all thy soul, and with all thy mind. This is the first and great commandment. And the second is like unto it, Thou shalt love thy neighbour as thyself. On these two commandments hang all the law and the prophets.

—Matthew 22:37–40

1570. In a positive learning environment, you don't have to become less, to become more. You should always maintain the dignity of what you bring to the table. You should never have to reduce yourself to increase yourself. Nor should you entertain anyone's expectation that you should. Who you already are brings richness to the new enriching experience.

The rich and poor meet together: the Lord is the maker of them all.

—Proverbs 22:2

1571. We should seek to gain wisdom in our relationships from our teachers and parents, because people die, but wisdom lives on. Wisdom is the principal thing.

Wisdom is the principal thing; therefore get wisdom: and with all thy getting get understanding.

—Proverbs 4:7

Also, that the soul be without knowledge, it is not good; and he that hasteth with his feet sinneth.

—Proverbs 19:2

Wisdom is good with an inheritance: and by it there is profit to them that see the sun. For wisdom is a defence, and money is a defence: but the excellency of knowledge is, that wisdom giveth life to them that have it.

—Ecclesiastes 7:11–12

1572. God has a special love for those who love Him back by obeying His principles in His Word, the Bible. Anyone who chooses to diligently follow the laws and principles of God's Word will receive the accumulating rewards of following after Him. You will be happy and blessed in the end!

I love them that love me; and those that seek me early shall find me. Riches and honour are with me; yea, durable riches and righteousness. My fruit is better than gold, yea, than fine gold; and my revenue than choice silver. I lead in the way of righteousness, in the midst of the paths of judgment: That I may cause those that love me to inherit substance; and I will fill their treasures.

—Proverbs 8:17–21

1573. When aimless people try to engage you into frivolous conversation, discreetly turn and walk away. It's not personal. It's just business. You're taking care of your own business. It's the key to outstanding success.

He that tilleth his land shall be satisfied with bread: but he that followeth vain persons is void of understanding.

—Proverbs 12:11

He that tilleth his land shall have plenty of bread: but he that followeth after vain persons shall have poverty enough.

—Proverbs 28:19

1574. The greatest way to witness to your unsaved loved ones and friends is by the love of God, the power of God, and your success. The love of God speaks, the power of God is powerful, and your success is what's evident. Evidence speaks the loudest.

Even so faith, if it hath not works, is dead, being alone. Yea, a man may say, Thou hast faith, and I have works: shew me thy faith without thy works, and I will shew thee my faith by my works.

—James 2:17–18

1575. The key to long-term success in marriage is that you can't think *single* when you're married. Marriage is about the two becoming one. When you're one, never think like you're

two again. Honor your marriage, and don't allow anyone else to dishonor it.

And he answered and said unto them, Have ye not read, that he which made them at the beginning made them male and female, and said, For this cause shall a man leave father and mother, and shall cleave to his wife: and they twain shall be one flesh? Wherefore they are no more twain, but one flesh. What therefore God hath joined together, let not man put asunder.

—Matthew 19:4–6

1576. People often act like they are the source of you having a big break! But God is the author of promotion. Promotion comes from God. If you do those things that qualify you for a big break, nothing or no one can restrain you!

For promotion cometh neither from the east, nor from the west, nor from the south. But God is the judge: he putteth down one, and setteth up another.

—Psalm 75:6–7

1577. The wife asked the husband, "What piece of the chicken can I have honey?" The husband answered, "You can have any piece you would like. The first man gave up a rib to get a good wife. I'm willing to give up any piece necessary to keep my 'good thing'."

And the Lord God caused a deep sleep to fall upon Adam, and he slept: and he took one of his ribs, and closed up the flesh instead thereof; And the rib, which the Lord God had taken from man, made he a woman, and brought her unto the man. And Adam said, This is now bone of my bones, and flesh of my flesh: she shall be called Woman, because she was taken out of Man. Therefore shall a man leave his father and his mother, and shall cleave unto his wife: and they shall be one flesh. And they were both naked, the man and his wife, and were not ashamed.

—Genesis 2:21–25

Whoso findeth a wife findeth a good thing, and obtaineth favour of the Lord.

—Proverbs 18:22

1578. When you get someone saved on Earth, you don't have to hear the trumpets on Earth to know that it's an important event and that there is a celebration. The angels in Heaven rejoice over every soul that is welcomed into The Body of Christ through salvation. Praise God! Saints, keep winning souls to Jesus!

Likewise, I say unto you, there is joy in the presence of the angels of God over one sinner that repenteth.

—Luke 15:10

The fruit of the righteous is a tree of life; and he that winneth souls is wise.

—Proverbs 11:30

1579. The key to maintaining our peace is to learn to live an uncomplicated life in the midst of a very complicated world. Jesus is the key to peace. Jesus is the answer.

Peace I leave with you, my peace I give unto you: not as the world giveth, give I unto you. Let not your heart be troubled, neither let it be afraid.

—John 14:27

1580. Bless The Lord, O my soul, *"and I gets all the benefits!"* As we bless The Lord, by making Him happy and to prosper in His will for the earth, we will get all the benefits! The Lord takes pleasure in our prosperity, as we seek His righteous cause, which is the salvation of all mankind, and the spread of His kingdom in the earth, which is righteousness, peace, and joy in The Holy Ghost!

Bless the Lord, O my soul: and all that is within me, bless his holy name. Bless the Lord, O my soul, and forget not all his benefits: Who forgiveth all thine iniquities; who healeth all thy diseases; Who redeemeth thy life from destruction; who crowneth thee with lovingkindness and tender mercies; Who satisfieth thy mouth with good things; so that thy youth is renewed like the eagle's.

—Psalm 103:1–5

Let them shout for joy, and be glad, that favour my righteous cause: yea, let them say continually, Let the Lord be magnified, which hath pleasure in the prosperity of his servant.

—Psalm 35:27

Beloved, I wish above all things that thou mayest prosper and be in health, even as thy soul prospereth.

—3 John 2

For the kingdom of God is not meat and drink; but righteousness, and peace, and joy in the Holy Ghost.

—Romans 14:17

1581. Believe God to live until 100 years of age or above. In that time, you have the power to rewrite the future of history.

And the Lord said, My spirit shall not always strive with man, for that he also is flesh: yet his days shall be an hundred and twenty years.

—Genesis 6:3

1582. The way to avoid being taken by surprise in life is to take nothing in life for granted. Pray about everything.

And he spake a parable unto them *to this end*, that men ought always to pray, and not to faint.

—Luke 18:1

Watch and pray, that ye enter not into temptation: the spirit indeed is willing, but the flesh is weak.

—Matthew 26:41

1583. When dark clouds seek to settle over your picnic, take the time to be the sunshine for someone else. Encourage others. Give, and it shall be given unto you!

Give, and it shall be given unto you; good measure, pressed down, and shaken together, and running over, shall men give into your bosom. For with the same measure that ye mete withal it shall be measured to you again.

—Luke 6:38

There is that scattereth, and yet increaseth; and there is that withholdeth more than is meet, but it tendeth to poverty. The liberal soul shall be made fat: and he that watereth shall be watered also himself.

—Proverbs 11:24–25

1584. Worship the Lord this morning! Let His praises be on your lips. Give thanks for His wonderful kindness. Exalt Him for His excellent grace. Experience His presence, by inviting Him into your room this morning. Praise Him! He's worthy to be praised by all His people. Let the saints lift up the song of the redeemed! For He is good, and His mercy endures forever!

Praise ye the Lord. Sing unto the Lord a new song, and his praise in the congregation of saints. Let Israel rejoice in him that made him: let the children of Zion be joyful in their King. Let them praise his name in the dance: let them sing praises unto him with the timbrel and harp. For the Lord taketh pleasure in his people: he will beautify the meek with salvation. Let the saints be joyful in glory: let them sing aloud upon their beds. Let the high praises of God be in their mouth, and a two-edged sword in their hand; To execute vengeance upon the heathen, and punishments upon the people; To bind their kings with chains, and their nobles with fetters of iron; To execute upon them the judgment written: this honour have all his saints. Praise ye the Lord.

—Psalm 149

1585. You can't hide quality, and you can't really fake it. You must develop it. Be the best at what God made you to do, and be the best you God made you to be, by continual self-development.

Seest thou a man diligent in his business? he shall stand before kings; he shall not stand before mean men.

—Proverbs 22:29

1586. You don't have anything else worth doing down here, but to fulfill your destiny. So, go ahead and fulfill it!

Pastor Terrance Levise Turner, MBA

Wherefore I perceive that there is nothing better, than that a man should rejoice in his own works; for that is his portion: for who shall bring him to see what shall be after him?

—Ecclesiastes 3:22

Whatsoever thy hand findeth to do, do it with thy might; for there is no work, nor device, nor knowledge, nor wisdom, in the grave, whither thou goest. I returned, and saw under the sun, that the race is not to the swift, nor the battle to the strong, neither yet bread to the wise, nor yet riches to men of understanding, nor yet favour to men of skill; but time and chance happeneth to them all.

—Ecclesiastes 9:10–11

1587. The bottom-line is, you have to keep on working, in order to impact the bottom-line.

In all labour there is profit: but the talk of the lips tendeth only to penury.

—Proverbs 14:23

In the morning sow thy seed, and in the evening withhold not thine hand: for thou knowest not whether shall prosper, either this or that, or whether they both shall be alike good.

—Ecclesiastes 11:6

1588. You've got to keep on fighting! Success doesn't go down easily! It won't fall at your feet without a struggle! But

keep on fighting, because success is guaranteed to the overcomer. And, you're more than a conqueror!

In all labour there is profit: but the talk of the lips tendeth only to penury.

—Proverbs 14:23

For a dream cometh through the multitude of business; and a fool's voice is known by multitude of words.

—Ecclesiastes 5:3

Nay, in all these things we are more than conquerors through him that loved us.

—Romans 8:37

1589. Think of yourself as an eternal person. Realize that everything you do and say has eternal impact. Therefore, be sure to make it count for something good!

While we look not at the things which are seen, but at the things which are not seen: for the things which are seen are temporal; but the things which are not seen are eternal.

—2 Corinthians 4:18

Either make the tree good, and his fruit good; or else make the tree corrupt, and his fruit corrupt: for the tree is known by his fruit. O generation of vipers, how can ye, being evil, speak good things? for out of the abundance of the heart the mouth speaketh. A good man out of the good treasure of the heart

bringeth forth good things: and an evil man out of the evil treasure bringeth forth evil things. But I say unto you, That every idle word that men shall speak, they shall give account thereof in the day of judgment. For by thy words thou shalt be justified, and by thy words thou shalt be condemned.

—Matthew 12:33–37

1590. Take the time to solve the problem. It will save you a lot of time.

The beginning of strife is as when one letteth out water: therefore leave off contention, before it be meddled with.

—Proverbs 17:14

The ear that heareth the reproof of life abideth among the wise.

—Proverbs 15:31

A prudent man foreseeth the evil, and hideth himself; but the simple pass on, and are punished.

—Proverbs 27:12

So teach us to number our days, that we may apply our hearts unto wisdom.

—Psalm 90:12

Boast not thyself of to morrow; for thou knowest not what a day may bring forth.

—Proverbs 27:1

1591. Jesus is the answer for today's world in which we live. He hasn't diminished in power. He hasn't diminished in influence. Through Him, you can be an overcomer in life. You can do all things through Christ, who strengthens you.

For whatsoever is born of God overcometh the world: and this is the victory that overcometh the world, even our faith.

–1 John 5:4

1592. Jesus is the answer for the world today. We must let the world know, in a language they can hear. The language is love and faithfulness.

For whatsoever is born of God overcometh the world: and this is the victory that overcometh the world, even our faith.

–1 John 5:4

By this shall all men know that ye are my disciples, if ye have love one to another.

—John 13:35

1593. It's good to have something of your own. Rather, than to be owned by something or someone else.

But let every man prove his own work, and then shall he have rejoicing in himself alone, and not in another.

—Galatians 6:4

Wherefore I perceive that there is nothing better, than that a man should rejoice in his own works; for that is his portion: for who shall bring him to see what shall be after him?

—Ecclesiastes 3:22

1594. Whatever may be your job today, work at it heartily. Be industrious. Be diligent. It's the key to upward mobility, recognition, and promotion.

And the man Jeroboam was a mighty man of valour: and Solomon seeing the young man that he was industrious, he made him ruler over all the charge of the house of Joseph.

−1 Kings 11:28

And Naomi had a kinsman of her husband's, a mighty man of wealth, of the family of Elimelech; and his name was Boaz. And Ruth the Moabitess said unto Naomi, Let me now go to the field, and glean ears of corn after him in whose sight I shall find grace. And she said unto her, Go, my daughter. And she went, and came, and gleaned in the field after the reapers: and her hap was to light on a part of the field belonging unto Boaz, who was of the kindred of Elimelech. And, behold, Boaz came from Bethlehem, and said unto the reapers, The Lord be with you. And they answered him, The Lord bless thee. Then said Boaz unto his servant that was set over the reapers, Whose damsel is this? And the servant that was set over the reapers answered and said, It is the Moabitish damsel that came back with Naomi out of the country of Moab: And she

said, I pray you, let me glean and gather after the reapers among the sheaves: so she came, and hath continued even from the morning until now, that she tarried a little in the house.

—Ruth 2:1–7

1595. The joy of The Lord is our strength. Take time to worship God with a heart of thanksgiving and praise. It will release the power of God on your behalf. Thanksgiving, praise, and worship are supernatural. It goes beyond the *natural* realm of reason, and releases God's *"super"* to work on your behalf!

It is a good thing to give thanks unto the Lord, and to sing praises unto thy name, O Most High: To shew forth thy lovingkindness in the morning, and thy faithfulness every night.

—Psalm 92:1–2

1596. The true wisdom of God has certain characteristics. Many Christians, who are proclaimed as wise, are wise in the ways of the world, and not the ways of God. Many Christians manage their lives by carnal strategies. However, the wisdom of God is pure, and without hypocrisy. It conveys the fruit of the spirit.

Most men will proclaim every one his own goodness: but a faithful man who can find?

—Proverbs 20:6

Who is a wise man and endued with knowledge among you? let him shew out of a good conversation his works with meekness of wisdom. But if ye have bitter envying and strife in your hearts, glory not, and lie not against the truth. This wisdom descendeth not from above, but is earthly, sensual, devilish. For where envying and strife is, there is confusion and every evil work. But the wisdom that is from above is first pure, then peaceable, gentle, and easy to be intreated, full of mercy and good fruits, without partiality, and without hypocrisy. And the fruit of righteousness is sown in peace of them that make peace.

—James 3:13–18

1597. When two steely willed individuals are married, it is so they can practice sharpening the blades of one another in love, while still being able to achieve progress. It is also so that when they enter into the real conflict outside of the safety of home, they can skillfully overcome evil with good, while continuing to walk in love.

Iron sharpeneth iron; so a man sharpeneth the countenance of his friend.

—Proverbs 27:17

Be not overcome of evil, but overcome evil with good.

—Romans 12:21

1598. Regarding helping people, don't do it because you have something to prove, do it because you have something to give.

As every man hath received the gift, even so minister the same one to another, as good stewards of the manifold grace of God.

–1 Peter 4:10

Or he that exhorteth, on exhortation: he that giveth, let him do it with simplicity; he that ruleth, with diligence; he that sheweth mercy, with cheerfulness.

—Romans 12:8

1599. Regarding problems, help it while you can help it. Address problems before they get out of hand. *"An ounce of prevention is worth a pound of cure!"*

The beginning of strife is as when one letteth out water: therefore leave off contention, before it be meddled with.

—Proverbs 17:14

A prudent man foreseeth the evil, and hideth himself; but the simple pass on, and are punished.

—Proverbs 27:12

Boast not thyself of to morrow; for thou knowest not what a day may bring forth.

—Proverbs 27:1

1600. Regarding the Bible, use it, and do it, rather than just *know* it. The Word of God was sent for our strategic use to be successful in life. Many people glory and argue about the deep meaning of scriptures, however, what's most important is to do it and use it for our strategic success.

Even so faith, if it hath not works, is dead, being alone. Yea, a man may say, Thou hast faith, and I have works: shew me thy faith without thy works, and I will shew thee my faith by my works.

—James 2:17–18

Beloved, I wish above all things that thou mayest prosper and be in health, even as thy soul prospereth.

—3 John 2

Final Word

Now that you have enjoyed *Distinguished Wisdom Presents... Living Proverbs–Volume 3*, I encourage you to read this book daily. Use it as a reference book for continual counsel. God's word is a healer. As you renew your mind to His Word you will be set free. Proverbs 4:7 says, "Wisdom is the principal thing; therefore get wisdom: and with all thy getting get understanding." Therefore, I recommend that you take time to read this book over again, and allow these truths to free you. Jesus said these words in John 8:31–32 and 36:

> Then said Jesus to those Jews, which believed on him, If ye continue in my word, then are ye my disciples indeed: And ye shall know the truth, and the truth shall make you free. If the son therefore shall make you free, you shall be free indeed.

God's Word is what makes us free. As we renew our minds to God's Word, our lives will be changed. We will enjoy the best that He desires for us. And we will be able to teach our children, grandchildren, and those that we come in contact with how to be free indeed. Therefore, as you read this book, *Distinguished Wisdom Presents... Living Proverbs–Volume 3*, my prayer is *May your life be enriched by the Words of wisdom!* Be sure to write a review of the book on the online sites you may have purchased the book from. Also, be sure to look for the

audiobook at www.TerranceTurnerLivingProverbs.com or Amazon.com. You will be further enriched as you hear the Words of the author in an audiobook. Thank you again for exploring this *treasury of wisdom*. God bless you.

Pastor Terrance Levise Turner, MBA

About The Author

Pastor Terrance Levise Turner is the senior pastor of Faith Country Holiness Church in Gallatin, TN. Pastor Turner has an MBA in Finance and Supply Chain Management, and a Bachelor's of Speech Communications and Theater/Mass Media from Tennessee State University. Pastor Turner is the author of several books, including the ***"Living Proverbs"***

series, and *Your Wealth Is In Your Anointing: Discover Keys To Releasing Your Potential.* His books and audiobooks are available at www.TerranceTurnerBooks.com. You can also find his daily blog and other books from the series at www.TerranceTurnerLivingProverbs.com. Terrance is also a singer/songwriter/recording artist. He ministers the gospel in Word and song with his wife, Avis. Their music is available at www.FaithCountryProductions.com. They live in Nashville, TN. Pastor Turner continues to serve the community and Body of Christ through service, music, and teaching the Word of God.

www.ingramcontent.com/pod-product-compliance
Lightning Source LLC
Chambersburg PA
CBHW030310080526
44584CB00012B/512